KT-386-793

Learning Through Child Observation

WITHDRAWN FROM

THE LIBRARY

UNIVERSITY OF
WINCHESTER

KA 0319427 2

of related interest

Kids Need...
Parenting Cards for Families and the People who Work With Them
Mark Hamer
ISBN 978 1 84310 524 4

A Multidisciplinary Handbook of Child and Adolescent Mental Health for Front-line Professionals
2nd edition
Nisha Dogra, Andrew Parkin, Fiona Gale and Clay Frake
ISBN 978 1 84310 644 9

Supporting Children and Families
Lessons from Sure Start for Evidence-Based Practice in Health, Social Care and Education
Edited by Justine Schneider, Mark Avis and Paul Leighton
ISBN 978 1 84310 506 0

The Social Worker's Guide to Children and Families Law
Lynn Davis
ISBN 978 1 84310 653 1

The Developing World of the Child
Edited by Jane Aldgate, David Jones, Wendy Rose and Carole Jeffery
Foreword by Maria Eagle MP
ISBN 978 1 84310 244 1

The Child's World
The Comprehensive Guide to Assessing Children in Need
Edited by Jan Horwath
ISBN 978 1 84310 568 8

Good Practice in Safeguarding Children
Working Effectively in Child Protection
Edited by Liz Hughes and Hilary Owen
ISBN 978 1 84310 945 7

Fun with Messy Play
Ideas and Activities for Children with Special Needs
Tracey Beckerleg
ISBN 978 1 84310 641 8

Quality Matters in Children's Services
Messages from Research
Mike Stein
Foreword by Helen Jones
ISBN 978 1 84310 926 6

Learning Through Child Observation

Second Edition

Mary Fawcett

Jessica Kingsley Publishers
London and Philadelphia

UNIVERSITY OF WINCHESTER
LIBRARY

First published in 2009
by Jessica Kingsley Publishers
116 Pentonville Road
London N1 9JB, UK
and
400 Market Street, Suite 400
Philadelphia, PA 19106, USA

www.jkp.com

Copyright © Mary Fawcett 2009

All rights reserved. No part of this publication may be reproduced in any material
form (including photocopying or storing it in any medium by electronic means and
whether or not transiently or incidentally to some other use of this publication)
without the written permission of the copyright owner except in accordance with
the provisions of the Copyright, Designs and Patents Act 1988 or under the terms
of a licence issued by the Copyright Licensing Agency Ltd, Saffron House, 6–10
Kirby Street, London EC1N 8TS. Applications for the copyright owner's written
permission to reproduce any part of this publication should be addressed to the
publisher.

Warning: The doing of an unauthorised act in relation to a copyright work may
result in both a civil claim for damages and criminal prosecution.

Library of Congress Cataloging in Publication Data
Fawcett, Mary, 1936-
    Learning through child observation / Mary Fawcett. -- 2nd ed.
        p. cm.
    Includes bibliographical references and index.
    ISBN 978-1-84310-676-0 (pb : alk. paper) 1. Social work with children--Great
Britain. 2. Family social work--Great Britain. 3. Participant observation. I. Title.
    HV751.A6F39 2009
    362.70941--dc22
                                  2009001771

British Library Cataloguing in Publication Data
A CIP catalogue record for this book is available from the British Library

ISBN 978 1 84310 676 0

Printed and bound in Great Britain by
Athenaeum Press, Gateshead, Tyne and Wear

For Trevor with love

UNIVERSITY OF WINCHESTER

03194272 155.4 FAW

3627

FAW

Acknowledgements

For more than 35 years, through contacts with students and colleagues in many different situations, my interest in the subject of observation has grown and deepened. It is almost invidious to single anyone out, but I must record my gratitude to Barbara Primmer (who first introduced me to child observation), Sonia Jackson (who encouraged me to write this book), and to all the 5x5x5=creativity community from whom I have learned so much in the last eight years. Particular thanks must go to social work colleagues – Margaret Boushel, Danielle Turney and Julie Selwyn – who have been such a support in the preparation of this second edition. I must record a special thanks to Susi Bancroft, Liz Elders, Ed Harker, Penny Hay and Andrea Sully whose thinking has inspired me in our collaborative work in 5x5x5=creativity. I am grateful to Sue Copping who assisted me with the drawing of Figure 5.1, 'a holistic view of the developing child', and to Liz Elders and Deborah Jones for Figure 9.1, the 'Creative and reflective cycle'. The various photographers, Linda Baker Smith, Penny Hay, Amy Houghton and Ed Harker, are very warmly thanked as are the teachers at St Stephen's Primary School and Twerton Infant School who also supported the project.

Any failings in this book are of course my sole responsibility.

Cover image: Bea painting at Batheaston School Bath, by Penny Hay.

Contents

Introduction

This second edition of *Learning Through Child Observation*, originally published in 1996, has been substantially revised and updated to allow for the changed UK context regarding the care and education of young children. Important new insights into aspects of observation are introduced from two sources, from Reggio Emilia in Italy and an arts-based educational project in UK with the name 5x5x5=creativity.

Learning Through Child Observation is a handbook designed for anyone working or preparing to work with children and their families in any of the children's services. The first edition appealed to staff in preschools, schools, social care, health and mental health, and this new edition is prepared with all these in mind. It is written in an accessible style in order to reach the wide range of people who work in this very large sector following the government's *Every Child Matters* agenda. Students of all ages (and their tutors) involved in the many courses and programmes that include observational studies will find practical guidance here about how to set up and carry out observations.

Observation is in some ways a simple and everyday idea yet at the same time it is profound and complex. *Learning Through Child Observation* examines this intriguing topic from many perspectives. It aims to help readers reach a deeper understanding of children and their lives as well as understanding themselves as adults engaged with children.

The first chapter looks at the many reasons why observation matters and also considers the current government legislation and priorities which establish the context for all staff working with children. Chapter Two, *Views on Children and Childhood*, is largely new for this edition. The aim is to raise awareness of the many and contrasting perspectives on children across time and place as well as among the professionals concerned. The observer's own habits of thinking about children and development are also considered here, as is the way in which perceptions about such topics as culture and gender are influenced by our own upbringing, education and experiences. The next chapter, *Changing Views of Child Observation*, offers a short overview of the history of child observation and contemporary views on some child development theories.

The subject of chapter Four is *Observational Methods and Practice*. Several methods, and examples with their various strengths and limitations, are set out. The purpose of this chapter is to help students, professionals or tutors in their selection of the most appropriate method for their particular task. The last section of this chapter turns to the evaluation of observational visits: what impact these sessions may have had on all the participants, the children, the parents, the staff, and the observers themselves. Chapter Five is titled *Child Observations: Themes and Lines of Enquiry* and follows on from the previous chapter. Here possible topics for study arising from observations are suggested, such as communication, attachment, concentration and schemas. *Preschool Contexts for Observation* in the UK, Chapter Six, focuses on the varied early years settings in which children are likely to be observed.

Observation and Assessment provides the focus of Chapter Seven. In the context of the government's *Common Assessment Framework* observation has a critical role to play. Staff in the various services for children will need to understand differing professional perspectives on the key tasks of assessment. The next chapter, *Supporting Child Observation*, is particularly targeted at lecturers or tutors planning course programmes that involve the practice and study of observation. The guidance will be useful for almost any programmes since it conveys much practical information, with some bias towards social work given the lack of material in this area.

Over the last eight years the author of this book has been engaged as consultant and evaluator of a UK research project, 5x5x5=creativity. The name originated in the first year when five artists began to work in five early years settings in collaboration with five cultural organisations (such as theatres, galleries and arts centres). The philosophy and practice of the preschools of Reggio Emilia in northern Italy was a major inspiration, but 5x5x5 has developed its own unique identity. It adopted the sub-title 're-searching children researching the world' and through deep engagement the author's own values about children's thinking, the arts and creativity across all ages have changed significantly. The last chapters concentrate on two important aspects of both of these approaches. Chapter Nine,

Observation, Reflection and Documentation: The Reggio Emilia Approach, sets out the linking steps between observation and documentation. The importance of reflective dialogue and collaborative practice is a key theme of this chapter. Chapter Ten, The *'Hundred Languages of Children'*, is complementary to the previous chapter. The recognition that there are many possible ways of expressing feelings and ideas is explored here assisted by case studies demonstrating the power of the 'hundred languages'. Clearly these examples are located primarily in educational settings, nevertheless, both chapters contain important material applicable to all areas of work with children and indeed other age groups.

The Appendix gives the task code categories from the Oxford Preschool Research Project (see Chapter Four and Five).

Throughout the book two important principles keep recurring. The first is the importance of valuing children, recognising their potential and competence, and really listening to what they have to say. The second is the significance of the wider setting of each child's life: family, community, culture, economic situation, geographical location, and even the wider influences that impact on their development.

Observation of children can be an endlessly fascinating, absorbing and revealing experience. As a tool for study it is richly interesting and almost always enjoyable. More than that, once the skills have been learned they are potentially useful across all work involving people, whatever their age or background.

CHAPTER ONE

Why Observation Matters

Observation is about taking children seriously, hearing what they have to say, respecting their interpretations, and valuing their imagination and ideas, their unexpected theories, their explorations of feelings and viewpoints. We can learn about children through watching and listening in an alert and informed way that raises awareness and sharpens understanding.

Of course we are noticing the world about us all the time. We must – for our own self-preservation. But what we take in is limited and necessarily selective. Observation means tuning in to children. In group settings with busy children and adults this can be difficult. In family situations where there are many demands on the observer's attention tuning in to the child can be hard. We often hurry to make a decision. We all have a tendency to see what we are looking for and to look for only what we know about. Rarely do we take time to stop and watch intently.

Observation raises many important issues. The observer's personal views about children are the result of their own childhood, professional background and the taken-for-granted ideas about children in our present culture. These factors contribute to the inevitable subjectivity of the observer. In addition, the circumstances of any observation – whether it is a normal everyday event or part of a more formal assessment process – affect the interpretations of the observer. Nor does the observation take place in a vacuum; the ecological detail of the environment and context all impact on the observer. We all have our own preconceptions, particular mindsets and prejudices stemming from our own cultural experiences, professional training, and the demands of the frameworks in which we work. Chapter Two examines this in detail.

UNIVERSITY OF WINCHESTER
LIBRARY

An example of the vital need for observation can be seen frequently in child abuse reports. Inevitably with every fresh tragic case of child abuse or death, social work staff are particularly under scrutiny for their part in the sad sequence of events. Often the reports call for children to be better 'seen and heard'.

However, we all need to learn how to observe effectively, how to focus systematically in an open-minded manner. The skills of observation, once learned, have relevance far beyond the immediate event.

The nature of observation

Observation does not exist in isolation – it is much more than a simple set of skills. We can learn much from our observations but we must accept that what we see is only the tip of the iceberg. Siraj-Blatchford (2009) explains that children's development cannot be reduced to its 'component parts' since much more is going on than can be observed. In early years settings there is a risk of classroom observations becoming very perfunctory. Isolated comments by children are sometimes recorded very briefly on 'post-it' notes, lacking either the context or the interactions between children. In other environments, observers from health and social care professions experience other barriers to sustained observation. They may give greater attention to the adults, who tend to demand more of their time, than the children.

The purposes of observation will vary. For example, teachers may use observational documentation, as described in Chapter Four, as a central element of the learning process in their class. Observations together with reflective dialogue among colleagues should be at the heart of everyday practice. Social workers similarly use observation as a regular tool but they will focus more on assessment procedures for children about whom there is concern. Medical colleagues need to maintain an observational alertness throughout their work. Observational knowledge and skills are therefore part of the initial training and preparation for students in all these fields. Observation will also often play a significant part in research for higher levels of study.

Skilled observers gather information in a systematic, detailed and precise way while recognising their own inevitable subjectivity. Through practice they acquire the ability to concentrate with full attention. For instance this may mean avoiding direct involvement in the observational setting. They are then learning how *to be* and not *to do*. Although it is possible to acquire such skills through individual practice alone, deeper understanding comes through focused learning about observation, and notably through subsequent reflection and discussion of the subject with others. The scope for learning afforded by observation is great and extends across various dimensions: practical skills, factual and theoretical knowledge, values and attitudes.

Among the practical skills that can be learned from observation is the ability to suspend judgement and to refrain from intervention. Preparation for observational sessions also teaches what recording methods and techniques are available, how to evaluate their strengths and limitations, and how to select the most suitable one for a particular task (see Chapter Four). The skills involved in setting up a series of observations responsibly are not insignificant, since they may include negotiation of the arrangement with staff and parents (including the sharing of information) and ensuring that the rights of the children and adults involved are respected. How to obtain young children's consent may be a thought-provoking task and should be undertaken with care.

Students may also learn through observation how anti-discriminatory principles can be put into practice, how power structures and hierarchies operate, and especially how relatively powerless children are in society. They can gain insight too into the dynamic of different situations and the effects of the observer's presence on the adults and children. Those new to working with children will learn the first stages in communicating with them. By discovering how to observe they begin to get a sense of 'where the children are', in other words the developmental stage they have reached, their individual perceptions and the worlds they inhabit. This can be an intriguing and empowering activity for the observer. Some have suggested it is like reading a novel in the sense that the observer seems to be following a plot.

Observation provides a rewarding opportunity to discover the subtle and fascinating ways in which people communicate, verbally and non-verbally, and about cultural differences in communication, for example the use of gestures, smiling, eye-contact, and through many other modes (see Chapter Two). Observation clearly has much to teach with regard to real children and their development in all its aspects: physical, social, emotional and cognitive. The observer learns how curious, sociable and intensely active young children are. Close observation may also reveal that the child being observed has some disability, developmental delay or particular need which has so far escaped detection. Observation can be especially valuable in helping students grasp the concept of a 'holistic' view of children – that is to say, the belief that children are not only complex and unique individuals but that the different strands of their development are inextricably bound up together and must all be taken into account.

Observation also helps students to understand theories of child development in context, evaluate them critically, and then use them as a tool to study a particular child. One theoretical framework proposes an 'ecological' view of each child as being part of a family with its own circumstances, which in turn is located within a cultural group, which itself belongs to a society at a particular moment in history (Bronfenbrenner 1979). This broader view focuses attention on both the social and economic circumstances of families and the effect of health and social policies laid down by central government and local authorities. Students engaged in planned observations should bear in mind this wider ecological context as well as the narrower one of the settings in which children often spend the greater part of their day.

All the same, observation is not purely a learning activity for students on courses, even though that may be the main reason for reading this text. It is an essential skill for anyone working with children in whatever capacity. For assessment of a child in everyday recording and documentation there is no alternative to observation. It is at the very heart of work with children.

In the area of personal learning observation can indeed be a profound experience, opening up undiscovered possibilities and helping to promote self-awareness. Students should be encouraged to recognise and examine their personal responses during observation, to reflect on the origin of such responses and, if necessary, deal with any dilemmas that arise. Within the student group, comparisons of observations bring home to participants the subjectivity of their own perceptions, as well as those of colleagues, and demonstrate how personal, even idiosyncratic, reactions often are. In the same way professionals of different backgrounds often find mutual discussion based on observational studies extremely revealing (Briggs 1992).

National context

Observation has climbed high on the agenda of necessary skills in work with young children over the last few years. How has this come about?

The Labour government that came to power in 1997 started the process of completely restructuring services for children with extensive quantities of new legislation from 2003 onwards. Pressures had been building for many years, based on unfavourable comparisons with our neighbours in Europe and on the serious gap between children who achieve and those who do not in our society. The government also perceived the need to ensure more single parents became earners in order to alleviate family poverty. The government had previously set up a very large research project, the *Effective Provision of Pre-school Education* (EPPE), charged with investigating the consequences of variations in the types of provision and the curriculum in the early years. EPPE's reports (Sylva *et al.* 2004) have been very influential in the profound rethinking of the state's involvement in children's and young people's experiences. The tipping point, however, might well have been the impact of the disastrous Climbié case (Laming 2003), in which a young African girl died in London at the hands of her aunt and her aunt's boyfriend when she had been sent to the UK by her parents in the hope of securing a better life.

This new approach for England (with slightly different versions in the other parts of the UK) starts from a set of five principles contained in the government's *Every Child Matters* agenda. This informs all the new structures, policies, practice and every aspect of professional development. Children are now entitled to five main 'outcomes':

- being healthy – enjoying good physical and mental health and living a healthy lifestyle

- staying safe – being protected from harm and neglect

- enjoying and achieving – getting the most out of life and developing skills for adulthood

- making a positive contribution – being involved with the community and society and not engaging in antisocial or offending behaviour

- achieving economic well-being – not being prevented by economic disadvantage from achieving their full potential in life.

Using this set of ECM outcomes the goal now is to bring together all professional services for children – childcare, education, health, social care and mental health – so that responsibility is integrated and children's safety and well-being can be ensured. To implement the vision and goals the government published a new document, *Choice for Parents, the Best Start for Children* (HMT 2004). Significantly, this ten-year strategy came from the Treasury. It charges local authorities with improving the outcomes for all children and narrowing the gap between those who achieve and those who do not. Accordingly every local authority now has its Children's Trust or Local Area Partnership led by a Director of Children's Services. Every type of early years service has now been incorporated into the overall plan but since state-provided early years provision was, and still remains, patchy and inadequate the private, voluntary and independent sector (PVI) is filling a very large gap.

The wide range of types of early years services – new children's centres, nursery schools, child minders, preschools (previously play-groups) and various other forms of provision – are now all under one leg-islative umbrella. Supporting them with large sums of public money, the government necessarily had to put in place some form of national standard. This has taken the form of the *Early Years Foundation Stage* (EYFS) for children from birth to five. From September 2008 every setting caring for and educating young children, including childminders, has had the statutory duty to follow these requirements. Inspections by Ofsted will enforce the law. In addition all children will be assessed through the EYFS Profile (www.standards.dfes.gov.uk).

The EYFS curriculum has drawn on the earlier government guidance laid out in *Birth to Three Matters* (2003) and the *Foundation Stage Guidance* (2000), but is specifically based on four themes and principles:

- a unique child
- positive relationships
- enabling environments
- learning and development.

Contained within the last theme, learning and development, are six topics:

- personal, social and emotional development
- communication, language and literacy
- problem-solving, reasoning and numeracy
- knowledge and understanding of the world
- physical development
- creative development.

Making these ambitious changes is a long-term project for the country and brings into focus several very challenging questions. Two of these are worth noting here. First, the integration of multi-professional teams is a very significant development, long called for in the light of high-profile cases of child abuse and ineffective working practices. The new partnerships have the potential to promote better co-operation leading to consistent goals. They should also aid collaboration – by jointly addressing issues (so avoiding overlap), allowing co-ordinated planning with shared goals, and improving service delivery (Anning *et al.* 2006; Siraj-Blatchford 2007). However, the challenges are many and complex. Not least is the development of a common language for discussion as professionals work together on an everyday basis and follow the set of special procedures from the government, the *Common Assessment Framework* (CAF), in cases where children are at risk or in need.

The second question concerns professional development as preparation for work and ongoing staff improvement. There are various levels and organisations tasked with ensuring the supply of qualified staff and establishing both initial and continuous professional development. In England the key body with these responsibilities is the Children, Young People and Families Workforce Development Council (CWDC). A *Common Core of Skills and Knowledge* has been defined and a single *Integrated Qualifications Framework* (IQF) is being developed.

In all the recent legislation affecting further and higher education and ongoing training programmes, observation will be an essential component. It is identified in every document as part of the communication skills that will be necessary to ensure that the aspirations of *Every Child Matters* are made a reality. Every team member will need to be knowledgeable about children's thinking, their progress, and the context of their lives. Observation skills and the concepts surrounding them are at the heart of this knowledge. There is a danger though that observation could be viewed as a foundational skill learned in initial professional education but that at higher levels, among more experienced people, there may be less need to give it attention. This is not the case. Observation is a vital research tool but also – especially when embedded in reflective dialogue with others (see Chapter Nine on documentation) – an endless source of information and constant stimulus to discovering how people of all ages think and relate to each other.

Time and again reports on child abuse tragedies have singled out the issue of professionals being insufficiently observant. For example, the report of the Cleveland affair (Noyes 1991) poignantly noted that every child must be seen above all as 'a person and not an object of concern' (p.iii). Further in his review of child death inquiries for the Department of Health, Noyes highlighted the need for greater awareness of the '*very existence of the child*' (my italics) (p.iii). It seems that in unduly stressful circumstances social workers tend to pay more attention to the adults than to the children. Too often, Phillips notes, social workers engaged in child protection do not pay sufficient attention to '*what is actually happening to the child*' (his italics) (Phillips 1988, p.32).

Professional development

Over the last few years there have been changes in initial vocational, professional training. In the case of social work education there was, in the past, a much stronger child development component. Now, as a broader, more generic programme has evolved, less time is being devoted to this topic. Other difficulties, which simply compound the time problem, include the lack of teaching staff with appropriate experience and the equal lack of suitable textbooks. There is a clear movement, however, towards re-establishing child observation and related study of child development as a central element. The whole subject is receiving more attention. See, for example, the journals *Infant Observation*, the *Journal of Social Work Practice* and the *Journal of Infant Mental Health* together with books such as *Observation and its Application to Social Work* (Le Riche and Tanner 1998) and *Direct Work: Social work with children and young people in care* (Luckock and Lefevre 2008). Observation also needs to be studied for its role in assessment, intervention and the focus on 'outcomes' when the impact of an intervention is scrutinised.

There are some moves to bring to the UK elements of the role of the 'social pedagogue', common in Europe. The principles of social pedagogy are primarily based on respect, children's rights, adults working creatively and collaboratively both together in teams and with children and young people, and seeing the child as a whole person – 'their mind, feelings, spirit and creativity' (Petrie *et al.* 2008, p.3). Two chapters in this book, on documentation (Chapter Nine) and on the hundred languages of children (Chapter Ten), link strongly with this pedagogical approach. Recently a course in Social Pedagogy has been established at the Institute of Education, University of London.

It is true that teacher education has now become primarily concerned with preparing teachers to deliver the National Curriculum. The concentration on specific curriculum subjects and the sequence of national testing of children currently dominate, and child development has thus been downgraded. It is now a minor topic, while even pedagogy (how to teach) has almost disappeared from training courses. Furthermore, the study of children under five is now very rare indeed in teacher education itself.

In stark contrast, other further and higher education courses give the early years priority, for example, degrees in Early Childhood Studies. There are now also Foundation Degrees and the Early Years Professional status courses that offer broader programmes with child development and observation given due attention.

At a more basic level there are the National Vocational Qualifications, and indeed a variety of other courses, all under the oversight of the Children, Young People and Families Workforce Development Council. The numbers of staff in the independent nursery sector have been increasing dramatically. However, this sector suffers from a very young and often inadequately trained personnel together with a very rapid turnover of staff. The National Vocational Qualifications and inspection systems probably ensure that basic standards are maintained. What seems to be lacking, though, is the development of the adults' deep perceptive understanding of children and the consequences of their own interactions in the daily care of young children (Elfer, Goldschmied and Selleck 2003).

CHAPTER TWO

Views on Children and Childhood

It can be salutary to consider the words people use to describe a 'child' or 'children' in general at this point in the early twenty-first century. There has been a tendency in the UK to see children as immature, irrational, incompetent, unsocialised beings, in comparison with adults who are presumed to be mature, rational, competent and socialised people. In this frame of thinking the key concept of childhood is one of development towards adult rationality and control. Indeed the study of child development and child psychology has in the past been dominated by the notion of the progression of the child from a state of 'not yet being' to becoming a fully 'grown up' and competent adult. As recently as 1991 Woodhead co-edited an important Open University text with the title *Becoming a Person* – a form of words, he now wryly notes, that implies children are not really people (Woodhead and Faulkner 2000).

What then is a child? What might be considered 'child-like' behaviour?

Preschool in Three Cultures: Japan, China and United States (Tobin *et al.* 1989) compared these three different cultures' views of children and their behaviour in preschool. Observations of videos made in the classes were discussed by preschool professionals from each country. One example, that of Hiroki, an energetic Japanese four-year-old who spent the morning commenting on all his tasks, making jokes, singing loudly, interrupting other children, poking them, punching and wrestling, provoked very different judgements. Among the comments, one American regarded the child as intellectually gifted but easily bored. The Chinese thought he was spoiled. The Japanese, while recognising he was 'challenging' to staff and children alike, remained unconcerned. The

Japanese class teacher in fact considered this behaviour appropriate for his age and simply called it 'child-like'.

This chapter investigates the shifting and varied perceptions of children and childhood by adults.

Historical perspectives

Looking back into history we find children represented in different ways as small adults, as wage-earners (part of the economy of the family), as untroubled innocents or alternatively even as sinners to be 'saved' through religion and physical punishment. Hendrick (1997) has categorised some of the different constructions placed on the notion of childhood. He instances 'the natural child' (the concepts of the philosophers John Locke and Jean-Jacques Rousseau), 'the romantic child' (popularised by the poet William Wordsworth), 'the wage-earning child', 'the delinquent child', and finally from the educationalist Hannah More 'the evangelical child' and so on. He demonstrates in fact the very large changes in attitudes to children over the last two hundred years. (See also Doddington and Hilton (2007) for a recent review of evolving perceptions of early childhood education over the same period.)

The observer's view of children and childhood

When we observe we are liable to think that we are seeing what anyone else would see. This is an illusion, for what we 'see' depends on what we bring to the observation in our own minds. We bring values and beliefs about ourselves, and about other people and the world that we may rarely discuss or even consciously consider. But students learning about children and observation (in every professional field) have a responsibility to examine their own attitudes very carefully, for these are bound to affect and limit observation. Furthermore, this development of self-awareness is also necessary in preparing for anti-oppressive practice in future professional work. We must recognise that we all have very personal definitions of our own selves, and that this personal definition includes our age, physical appearance, gender and sexual orientation, ethnic or national origin, class and religion. In addition, we need to consider how we relate to other people. This means understanding where we belong in society, what personal power we have, and how we perceive those with different attitudes and values. Finally, we must inform ourselves about structural oppressions in society.

Reflection on the source of our personal understandings and beliefs is a productive first step. We can start by recalling our own childhood. The effects of the rules, roles and 'indoctrination' we all experienced as children almost certainly linger on (though we may react strongly against them). They may influence our adult notions about, say, the smacking and punishment of children, our attitudes towards food, our ideas about appropriate dress, possibly bias towards or against some groups in society – even our suspicions and intolerance of disability or mental illness. Outside the family, our schooling will itself have been responsible for forming opinions. Did we share the playground with children of all social classes? Were we at a single-sex school? Was the local dialect regarded as inferior and therefore to be eradicated?

Looking back on these early experiences it is well to remember, as J.P. Hartley famously wrote in the novel *The Go-Between*, 'The past is another country.' For many people the changes in the last 50 years have been the greatest ever known in a lifetime. Women's roles, family structures, lifestyles and life expectancy have been transformed. The availability of personal transport, television, computers and gadgetry of all kinds has altered many people's life experiences and consequently their perceptions. We need, though, to be very aware of the continuing power and influence of the media (the press, television, cinema, etc.) in shaping our views, especially as regards the portrayal of children and childhood in a way that may deny reality. The media may for example fan prejudice or cause an outcry about the failings of social workers and children's services. The storm over Baby P in November 2008 is a case in point. Unpicking this tragedy may reach back to the roots of adults' violence. Growing up in a childhood environment of violent abuse or neglect and consequent anxiety is psychologically damaging. It is also known to be physiologically harmful too since anxiety affects brain development through the over-production of adrenaline (Johnson 2007).

The notion of childhood as a period of both innocence and ignorance is still too often assumed and accepted by the general public. In fact children as young as three are quite clear about gender and racial difference, and they may well have witnessed scenes of sexual intercourse, violence and death on the television screen. By the age of five they know the values society ascribes to women and girls or to different skin colours (Siraj-Blatchford 1994). Public attitudes towards children and their developmental needs are also moulded by fashionable media perspectives. Even the specialised literature can mislead and must be treated with sceptical caution. Frequently the 'holistic' standpoint – i.e. the complex totality of the human experience – has simply not been properly acknowledged. Moreover, the Western norms of child development have all too often been prioritised and used indiscriminately.

The next section of this chapter aims to alert the reader to some areas of potential bias. It is not comprehensive and students should read more widely and share these topics in discussion with others. Culture, language, physical appearance and gender are the four topics considered here. There may be some overlap, but investigating them one at a time may help to clarify understanding.

Cultural perspectives

Culture is an overused word with many shades of meaning. In this context it will be taken to mean a 'shared pattern of living'. As such it is not static but continually evolving. It includes class and shared religious beliefs. There is a tendency to focus on the more familiar tokens of culture that we all inherit – customs, dialect, music and songs, myths and legends, food and clothing, household goods – but just as important, though perhaps less obvious, is the 'shared total communication framework'. Within our cultural group we share not just the spoken and written words of our language, but also gestures and actions, tones of voice and facial expressions. These different aspects of communication are always present but they remain 'invisible' as long as we stay within our familiar culture. We employ them subconsciously. But when observing or communicating with members of other cultures we are more likely to notice such traits. In her book *Multicultural Issues in Child Care* (1993), Janet Gonzalez-Mena urged the importance of developing sensitive observational skills if we want to be good at communicating with children and adults. She picked out five areas in which students need to learn these skills, even though they may share a common spoken language with the children and adults in the observational setting. These concern smiling, eye-contact, sensitivity to personal space, touch, and time concepts. The frequency of smiling is very variable across cultures. Russians tend to smile only in the context of humour, rather than use it as a friendly overture. During Cold War exchanges, the broad smile of the American greeting was taken by the Russians as evidence either that the other side lacked intelligence or that the smile was fake. On the other hand the Americans thought the

Russians cold and unfriendly. In some Asian and African cultural groups eye-contact between adults would be seen as insolence, whereas to some English people a lack of eye-contact is interpreted as shiftiness. People from rural and urban districts may have very different expectations of appropriate personal space. Pease (1981, p.23) reports on the problems encountered in Australia by a Danish couple whose behaviour was considered to be overtly sexual because of their close body contact. The difficulty was that Europeans typically are comfortable with a personal space of 20–30 centimetres, while for Australians the comparable figure is more like 46 centimetres, so the close proximity of the Danes was misinterpreted. Some rural people may feel happier with a much greater personal zone, as much as six metres, according to Pease.

Every cultural group has its own shared patterns of family up-bringing and likewise particular goals for its children. The small snapshot of Hiroki at the start of this chapter indicates different cultural perspectives on children's behaviour in preschool settings. Another example is the taken-for-granted, middle-class, Western practice of placing babies to sleep alone in a separate room. This is seen as cruel in some other cultures, contrasting strongly with their own expectation that an infant should naturally sleep with the mother. Styles of bringing up children are not immune to change. Within a generation customs may be transformed as a result of education, the redefining of women's roles, the commercial availability of goods and conveniences, and changing work patterns.

Language

The observer's views about language use may well be influenced by views in society on the status of different languages. In the UK Western languages such as French still seem to be held in higher regard than the home languages of ethnic communities (Urdu, for example). The attitude to bilingualism is curious. In 1994 Siraj-Blatchford wrote 'in British education and care systems being bilingual is still too often perceived as an aberration, or worse, as something children should grow out of' (Siraj-Blatchford 1994, p.46). When one considers that over 70 per cent of the world's people use more than one language in their daily lives this narrow perspective is depressing. Children whose first language at home is not English are thus seen as both *being* and *having* a problem when the evidence is that learning two languages is beneficial to the speaker.

Bilingualism actually helps the development of English (Hazareesingh, Simms and Anderson 1989). For one thing learners become more aware of the fact that names seem quite arbitrary (a dog can also be called *un chien*). They also become more alive to emotional expressions (e.g. they are better able to interpret facial expressions, gestures and tone of voice) and have greater social sensitivity and improved concept formation. Bilingualism should rather be seen as a strength, and valued as such. (Siraj-Blatchford (1994) provides a very useful chapter on the subject.)

Dialect seems to be acceptable in varying degrees too. A hierarchy can be discerned here so that the accents of rural Aberdeenshire or Devon, for instance, tend to be preferred to the urban voices of Glasgow and Birmingham. There are notions too about what constitutes 'good' and 'bad' English – notions that are subtly changing all the time because language is not static, it evolves.

In the observation of small children, expectations about developmental progress may colour perceptions. Apparent mispronunciations (sometimes sentimentalised and regarded as 'cute') are very common. Two instances of this typical developmental stage are 'wabbit' for rabbit and 'fis' for fish. Children often over-apply certain grammatical forms, such as the -ed ending of the past tense, e.g. 'I went to the shops and *buyed* some biscuits.' This is actually an indication, of course, that the child understands the principle of forming the past tense rather than a mistake. (Language is one of the themes for study in Chapter Five.)

Physical appearance

Beauty may be only skin-deep, but the 'image', the outer appearance, influences our impression of a person. Healthy, properly nourished, well-groomed, alert young children are very appealing. For survival the human infant must be 'attractive' to the caring adults, so the 'baby' features of chubby face, big wide eyes and soft skin are part of nature's way of ensuring the interest of the adults. Some adults are especially charmed by the beauty and seeming innocence of children. The young of all ethnic groups can possess this quality. On the other hand, some children do not have an aura of loveliness. They may seem dull and lifeless, awkward, unkempt, thin and miserable. Two further characteristics of children's appearance that may influence the observer are size and apparent maturity. Some children look much older or younger than they really are. All these factors can very forcefully affect adults' perceptions and expectations of children. We may be at risk of condoning unaccept-able behaviour, or not believing that a child is capable of doing some-thing unkind, because that child looks so beautifully innocent. The opposite may well result too, so that the lacklustre child is not credited with achievements. It is well known that children who appear older than their true age can be at a serious disadvantage when behaviour does not meet expectations.

Observers and workers with young children may well find them-selves drawn to some children rather than others, though they will of course try to maintain an even-handed, professional stance. If a child has to be selected for an observation exercise it is therefore best to find some way of randomising the choice – perhaps by selecting the first child who comes in wearing something blue, or taking a letter from the alphabet and finding the first name on the list starting with that letter.

'Race' is a word that needs defining, even though so-called racial characteristics are entirely trivial and only 'skin-deep'. The word refers purely to physiological difference – skin colour, hair type and the like. But while these characteristics are quite superficial, they have long been used, and still are, to group people and to grant them greater or lesser status accordingly. As Iram Siraj-Blatchford put it in 1994:

> White scientists invented racial categories and, given the history of white domination and exploitation of black people, they put themselves at the top of their racial hierarchy…most British people still believe or act according to this racist structure. (Siraj-Blatchford 1994, p.4)

Much racism is still unrecognised, covert and insidious, and because it is fundamentally to do with power (prejudice in combination with power creates racism) it is particularly dangerous and difficult to counter and eradicate. Gambe *et al.* (1992), in a training manual for social workers, have drawn attention to three areas of risk – *exclusion* (i.e. ignoring the existence of 'race', claiming to be 'colour-blind' and stating that 'I treat them all the same'); *tokenism* (i.e. paying attention to 'race' only as an after-thought); and *pathology* (in seeing other groups as strange, different and inferior). This last area is most significant in observation. Owusu-Bempah (1994) investigated the hypothesis that 'Many people seem to accept, as self-evident, the notion that black children harbour unfavour-able cognitions about themselves and their racial group, and that they would rather be white' (Owusu-Bempah 1994, p.123). He found the myth to be still widespread among social work students, for example.

Interpretations of children's behaviour and needs may still reflect the dangerous misconception of negative self-concepts. To suggest that black children's friendships with white children are 'pathological', as may happen, is clearly unhelpful. By viewing children in this way there is a strong risk of self-fulfilling effects and a compounding of latent difficulties. Concepts of self and attitudes within communities are not static. Many young black British people have generally positive self-images, especially in the more multicultural areas of Britain. Meanwhile more isolated members of minority groups may indeed harbour negative feelings about themselves. Observation studies should give students the opportunity to consider these issues and to observe behaviour as objectively as possible, listening very carefully to what children and adults are really saying.

Gender

Early years settings, where some children spend the greater part of their day, are not small oases apart from the 'real' world. Attitudes and behaviour with regard to women and men in the outside world do impinge. And of course at the preschool stage the gender imbalance among the preschool staff is especially evident. Responsibility for the education and care of the youngest children is traditionally seen as women's work and the task is overwhelmingly apportioned to women within the individual family, but also in society at large. It may well be the case that women are rather better suited to the very diverse, responsive multi-tasking types of skill that are required. Women are usually more comfortable with a nurturing and holistic approach, while staff in early years settings inescapably find themselves switching rapidly between very basic physical, caring roles and responding to more intellectual challenges and stimulation. Some men, though not all, may feel ill at ease in the practical caring for young children or they may prefer to concentrate on single defined tasks rather than be constantly switching their attention. But there are other reasons too for the lack of males in preschool employment. It is perceived as low status, poorly paid and lacking in promotion prospects, and primarily (as noted above) as 'women's work'. Women are likely to have similar views. It is increasingly clear that the status of workers, of either gender, with this age group should be improved and that their special characteristics, skills and achievements better valued. Education and care with small children deserves to be properly rewarded, with a clear career path, in order to ensure higher self-esteem, confidence and a proper sense of professionalism.

Yet there is more to the gender issue in early years settings than the serious absence of men (with the message that this gives) and the consequent lack of male role models for children at a developmentally crucial stage (see the section on gender differences in Chapter Five). The very nature of the resources chosen, the activities, and the attitudes of the staff may all influence children's perceptions of gender roles. Early years settings tend to be conservative, traditional places. Stereotyping is not necessarily confronted and staff do not always realise how their choices of equipment, say, or their responses to children can have long-term consequences.

The allocation of tasks by requests such as: 'Which big, strong boys are going to help me shift the computer?' or 'I need some girls to tidy up the home corner' are not at all uncommon. Staff perceptions of boys and girls are widely different. Boys are seen as dynamic but posing more problems, whereas girls are viewed more favourably as being easier to manage. Moreover, staff reactions are likely to reinforce the girls' reticence and the boys' confidence. (See also Chapter Five.)

As suggested above, the selection of resources for children will also shape their play experiences and reinforce social conditioning. 'Action man' and 'Barbie doll' (still selling many millions around the world every year) symbolise the potency of toys that stereotype. In *Playing them False* Dixon (1989) revealed how seemingly uncontroversial play equipment is part of 'big business' and a force to be reckoned with. In addition pictures, posters and the content of a surprising number of traditional stories are all possible sources of stereotyped gender roles. From a somewhat different angle it is known that the more spatial activities that boys are engaged in stimulate their scientific and mathematical understanding, while the emphasis on the social interaction of girls' play improves their language, and in turn their literacy skills. Gurian (2001) gives a clear account of the differences between boys' and girls' brains from the start of their lives. He also suggests the kinds of activities that support and extend children of both sexes. We know already that preschool experiences affect later development and achievement, but we still need to know more about how to enhance the outcomes.

UNIVERSITY OF WINCHESTER
LIBRARY

Professional bias

While many readers of this book will just be starting out on a professional career, others may have been working with children and families for some years. In the course of professional preparation one is bound to absorb the priorities, ethos, methods and styles of problem solving of that profession, as well as learning a particular way of viewing the people one is responsible for. Training, as it should, does make a difference. An interprofessional group engaged in in-service training will find a rich vein for discussion by comparing their sometimes divergent interpretations of observed behaviour. In one actual case, a mixed group of nursery teachers and nursery nurses were shown an illustration of a young child standing on a high stool wielding a pair of scissors while cutting some foliage (illustrated in Drummond, Rouse and Pugh 1992, section one, image eleven). Analysing their reactions to the illustration, they were sharply divided according to their training backgrounds. The teachers concentrated approvingly on the pleasure and interest the child displayed in the imaginative activity, while the nursery nurses felt the child was not being adequately safeguarded by the adults, and was at risk of falling and being hurt by the scissors. Social workers, health staff, psychologists, teachers and so on will all have different viewpoints and interests. This topic will be considered further in Chapter Seven which looks at assessment, where this word itself has different meanings across the professions.

Views of children in educational settings

In the UK anxiety about educational standards and achievement seems to be increasing and is often the focus of the media. Parents, especially middle-class ones, typically feel pressured to make their child-rearing conform with the prevailing trend. In 1991 Hallden researched parents' attitudes in Sweden and found opposite viewpoints that emphasised either the *child as being* or the *child as project*. In the first concept – the child as being – development is seen as a natural process directed by inner drives. The child's development is not something to be speeded up and the role of the parents is therefore to be a resource always available to their children. 'The parents do not measure their children in terms of a "normality timetable"'. In the second concept – the child as project – the parental approach is combined with 'the societal myth of the possibility of directing, controlling and planning human life' (Hallden 1991, p.344).

The notion of moulding children and even social engineering through education can be seen in any country's educational programme. A government's philosophical attitude to children and its views of the purpose of education will shape the legislation. Sometimes one needs to read between the lines, but generally the official language used will reveal the underpinning philosophy and objectives. The following section outlines a few national and regional policies.

New Zealand

Te Whaariki, the New Zealand curriculum for the early years, has its roots in Maori culture and takes a holistic view of the child in the community (New Zealand Ministry of Education 1996). The values of the community are evident in the four principles: empowerment, holistic development, family and community, and relationships. The curriculum is seen as a tapestry (the word Whaariki means a woven mat) where the strands are well-being, belonging, contribution, communication and exploration. Children progress across these areas rather than, as it were, climbing a ladder. There is a strong emphasis on play and discovery, allowing children to develop at their own pace. In other words children are valued as individual 'beings', not as 'projects' in Hallden's terminology. The form of assessment used is very different from that in the UK (discussed below). In New Zealand they have developed 'Narrative Assessment' (Kei Tua o te Pae; see www.educate.ece.govt.nz/programmes) which emphasises the recording of children's actual achievements by creating portfolios for each child.

Scandinavia

Throughout Scandinavia the early years are considered to be much more important for the development of children as *people* rather than as preparation for becoming a *schoolchild*. In England the Office for Standards in Education's report (Ofsted 2003) comparing six-year-olds in English schools with those of Denmark and Finland found that the Scandinavians gave higher priority to personal and social development, learning how to learn, and developing self-control. In English schools literacy and numeracy took up much more time and tended to dominate the curriculum.

Reggio Emilia, northern Italy

The influence of the northern Italian city of Reggio Emilia can be seen worldwide (see Chapter Nine). Loris Malaguzzi's guidance and thinking, as an educationalist and psychologist, were profoundly important in the evolution of the philosophy and educational practice of the Reggio preschools. The underpinning values of this system explicitly depend on an 'image of the child as strong, powerful, and rich in resources, right from the moment of birth' (Rinaldi 2006, p.12). In this city the child is understood as an active agent in his or her own learning, including the very definition of the curriculum. Given this view of children as competent, creative and active in constructing their own knowledge Reggio professionals and parents believe that listening to all the children's communications is the very bedrock of their pedagogy, or way of teaching. In other words they believe in a 'listening pedagogy' (Rinaldi 2006) to guide their curriculum. The priority Reggio gives to the arts as an integral part of education by employing an artist as a full-time member of staff indicates the value given to seeing children as creative learners. Malaguzzi has put it this way:

> Once children are helped to perceive themselves as authors or inventors, once they are helped to discover the pleasures of inquiry, their motivation and interest explode … to disappoint the children deprives them of possibilities that no exhortation can arouse in later years. (Edwards, Gandini and Forman 1998, pp.67–68)

Wales

The Welsh administration has taken an independent and different approach to education legislation from that in England, as has Scotland. A concept of children as active, playful individuals is the starting point of the new foundation stage curriculum for three- to seven-year-olds in Wales (Welsh Assembly Government 2008). Children are expected to learn through first-hand experiences, through play and active involvement. 'It is important that children are not introduced to formal methods of learning too soon as this can have a detrimental effect on their future learning and development' (p.10). The guidance is based on many case studies and says, for example, that children are to be engaged in developing their own outdoor play areas (outdoors experience being thought highly valuable). When asked what they would like to see and do in their

outdoor play area the children responded 'birds, an aeroplane, a play house, raspberries and lots of flowers' (p.11).

England

There is no doubt that the English *Every Child Matters* agenda (Department for Education and Skills 2003) has been strongly influenced by the UN Convention on the Rights of the Child (United Nations 1989), while the new *Early Years Foundation Stage* (EYFS) also reflects elements of the New Zealand and Reggio approaches. That said, the admirable four themes of the EYFS doctrine – a unique child, positive relationships, enabling environments, and learning and development – seem not to be fully followed through in the detail of the present guidance, since various contradictions betray very different views of children and the purpose of education. In particular children are considered to be *pupils* from a very early stage. The emphasis seems to be essentially on academic achievement in schools and in the early years.

The idea that even the very early years should be a time of preparation for school – where children will be expected to attain specific literacy and numeracy goals – is given considerable space. These desired academic skills are presented in a logical ladder-like progression. But the notion of the unique child able to develop at her own pace and in her own way is not compatible with this rather prescriptive approach. Though the EYFS literacy and numeracy objectives are described as 'guidance', the culture and expectations that currently prevail in English schools mean that staff feel judged and their school rated, as indeed it will be. There is a serious issue here – the clash between the *Every Child Matters* agenda and the new early years curriculum. Perhaps a new curriculum altogether is required that would bring together all the different philosophical and professional perspectives.

In conclusion a pertinent quote:

> Social workers, judges, government ministers, child killers, paedophiles, psychiatrists and parents were all children once. Each and every one of us carries our own, usually well hidden and frequently denied, emotional and irrational baggage relating to our own subjective experiences of having once been a child. (Gittins 1998, p.2)

CHAPTER THREE

Changing Views of Child Observation

Historical perpsectives

Observation has a long history. Thoughtful observers of animal and human life have given us great art, from the prehistoric cave painters to artists of our own age. Scientists too have long been careful observers of the world around them and have developed and improved ways of seeing it. They have extended the limits of the human eye, for example, with ingenious devices like microscopes, telescopes, X-rays, sensors and ultra-sonic scanners. Cameras and video recorders have added another dimension. We can now see events over and over again.

The recording of children's behaviour is also not a new idea, but has a notable tradition. The simplest form of observation record is the diary entry. Parents and others from different backgrounds have noted children's progress and activities for centuries. All that was necessary was writing ability and motivation. Typically the first smile, the appearance of teeth, when the child first walked, or accounts of illnesses were all documented.

Such very personal, anecdotal records may be fascinating and offer insights into a family's private life, but these are single cases and not necessarily a guide to other people's experiences. Clearly the subject has not been randomly selected from the general population, nor picked out as a representative of a particular group. The infant or child is being observed simply as a precious individual, a special member of the family.

From at least the seventeenth century books have been appearing that offer guidance on how to bring children up properly and how to train and educate them. A change in attitude is detectable from the later eighteenth century under the influence of Jean-Jacques Rousseau's writings. Rousseau believed that children's natural development should be recognised and fostered, and that the didactic practices of adults at that time might be harmful. In his view the behaviour of the child was a legitimate area of study in its own right. One of the first significant publications after Rousseau's ground-breaking book *Émile, or On Education* (1975, first published in 1762) was the work of a Swiss theorist, Johann Heinrich Pestalozzi (1746–1827), who in 1774 published a record of his son's early development. A decade or so later, in Germany, Dietrich Tiedeman similarly produced a written account of *his* son's first three years. What should be recognised here is that these were books of a new kind, and led to a realisation in the nineteenth century that the child is a thinking person worthy of study and investigation, and that natural behaviour is a valuable aid to understanding the child's mind. From now on presumptions about the nature of children, and how they should be educated, trained and disciplined, would increasingly be argued over.

Perhaps the greatest stimulus to child study was the work of Charles Darwin (1809–1882). It is hard for us now to appreciate the tremendous impact of his book *On the Origin of Species* (1859). 'If a new sun had appeared in the sky, the astonishment of educated men from San Francisco to Moscow, from Melbourne to Bergen, could hardly have been greater than it was then' (Preyer quoted in Kessen 1965, p.131). While this seminal work was in gestation, Darwin was closely observing his own children, especially his first-born, 'Doddy' (William Erasmus Darwin). His acute observations reveal a very sensitive observer as well as an affectionate father. The motives for the record-keeping went beyond those of an interested, loving parent. He was deliberately looking for parallels between primitive man and the modern child – indeed he believed that in a developing child he was seeing the process of evolution itself. His subsequent studies comparing humans with other species, presented in *The Expression of Emotions in Man and Animals* (1872), drew directly on these observations of children, though the actual records of Doddy's early life were not finally published until 1887, some 37 years after he had made them. He was prompted to make public his observations of his son's first three years after reading the French philosopher and historian Hippolyte Taine's account of the mental development of an infant. Darwin's response to this, and to another new description of Wilhelm Preyer, a physiologist, was to publish an article 'A biographical sketch of an infant' in the journal *Mind* (1877):

During the first seven days various reflex actions, namely sneezing, hiccoughing, yawning, stretching, and of course sucking and screaming, were well performed by my infant. On the seventh day, I touched the naked sole of his foot with a bit of paper, and he jerked it away, curling at the same time his toes, like a much older child when tickled. The perfection of these reflex movements shows that the extreme imperfection of the voluntary ones is not due to the state of the muscles or of the coordinating centres. At this time, though so early, it seemed clear to me that a warm soft hand applied to his face excited a wish to suck. This must be considered as a reflex or an instinctive action, for it is impossible to believe that the experience and association with the touch of his mother's breast could so soon have come into play. During the first fortnight he often started on hearing any sudden sound, and blinked his eyes. The same fact was observed in some of my other infants within the first fortnight. Once, when he was sixty-six days old, I happened to sneeze, and he started violently, frowned, looked frightened, and cried rather badly: for an hour afterwards he was in a state which would be called nervous in an older person, for every slight sound made him start. (Darwin, quoted in Kessen 1965, p.118–119)

In the same article he hypothesised about gender-specific behaviour in the same child who, at two years three months, had been throwing books and sticks at:

anyone who offended him; and so it was with some of my other sons. On the other hand, I could never see a trace of such aptitude in my infant daughters; and this makes me think that a tendency to throw objects is inherited by boys. (Darwin, quoted in Kessen 1965, p.121)

He also made comparisons with animals, contrasting the expression of jealousy in children and dogs.

Darwin's fame brought the 'baby biography' to public attention. Here was an important method for the study of children that was academically respectable. Nevertheless, another child study published by Wilhelm Preyer, based on the first three years of *his* son's life, is generally agreed to be the first proper child study, even if not wholly accurate. Kessen describes Preyer as setting a pattern for child study. Even though Preyer made some surprising errors, for example he wrote 'All children immediately after birth are deaf ', nevertheless his reports are subtle, if at times confusing (Preyer quoted in Kessen 1965, p.143). But his fine observation of another child, unusually a girl, is also worth quoting:

A little girl in the eleventh month found her chief pleasure in 'rummaging' with trifles in drawers and in little boxes ... the eagerness and seriousness with which such apparently aimless movements are performed, is remarkable... This is not mere playing, although it is so-called; it is *experimenting.* (his italics) (Preyer, quoted in Kessen 1965, p.143)

The next significant figure was the American psychologist Granville Stanley Hall (1846–1924). His child study, *The Content of Children's Minds* (1883), went beyond observation, since he chose to question the children themselves. Child questionnaires henceforth became a fashionable new tool for information-gathering. Hall's work gave a powerful impetus to the development of child psychology especially in the USA. He had a deep interest in children 'as they really are'. Some of the quality of this commitment is revealed in a paper with the title 'The Story of a Sand Pile', which documents his observations of a group of children when presented with a large load of sand. His curiosity about this episode centres particularly on the children's creative and vigorous response to this interesting opportunity for 'digging, exploring, constructing, destroying'. (Hall quoted in Kessen 1965, p.150). Among his many initiatives Hall introduced the writings of Wilhelm Preyer, mentioned above, to the American public, encouraging mothers to follow Preyer's example and keep records of their own infant's development. He also brought Sigmund Freud over from Europe on a lecture tour.

By 1900 child study had become an essential tool in the investigation of human development, used by professionals and the general public alike. The drive to make it even more scientific led to the establishment of special child study centres at universities across the USA. Parents were requested to bring their children to laboratory nursery schools so that observations could be conducted in controlled surroundings. Psychologists and educationalists were becoming deeply interested in the early years of childhood and their potential significance. They wanted to discover the 'normal' sequence of development. A specialised journal, *Child Study Monthly,* was launched in the 1890s.

Nonetheless, critics of the laboratory-based, controlled experiments with small children began to voice their scepticism and to publish alternative studies. Anthropologists, most famously Margaret Mead, went out into the natural environment collecting evidence for their case studies (or field studies as they called them). Their criticism of laboratory studies seems obvious to us now, for the behaviour of young children must be

affected, even distorted, by placing them in an unusual environment. Barker and Wright, two American 'ecological psychologists', appreciated not only that behaviour outside the laboratory would be quite different but also that experimental research on children typically carried out by psychologists bore little relation to what children were familiar with in their daily lives. By contrast, Barker and Wright's classic study, *One Boy's Day* (1951), is precisely what it suggests. They had attempted to document, without any interference, the natural stream of behaviour of one seven-year-old boy from the moment he got up to when he went to bed. The authors argued that, though it can be very difficult for observers to avoid altering the phenomenon they are investigating, children are particularly unselfconscious and will probably not display uncharacteristic patterns of behaviour for any length of time. The snag with naturalistic observation is the problem of organising the enormous quantity of data generated. Its great strength, though, is that it does portray the full range and complexity of behaviour. This account demonstrates the importance of noting the child's real habitat – the location, the presence of other people, and the expectations and rules under which the child is operating. It is an example of an *ecological* approach.

Back in Europe observations were also being made which have had long-term consequences on the way children are viewed. Sigmund Freud (1856–1939) proposed various highly influential theories, based on his own observations, about the development of personality and the significance of early experiences. Valid or otherwise, these have since become part of everyday 'knowledge'. In Switzerland Jean Piaget (1886–1980) kept records of his three children's behaviour from when they were newly born. He was virtually a child prodigy himself, publishing his first academic article (on bird behaviour) in a learned journal by the age of 14. Though originally a biologist and zoologist, Piaget became intrigued by the way young human beings seem to construct their own understanding of the world. The study of epistemology (the development of knowledge and understanding) absorbed him throughout his long and productive life.

In Britain the work of Susan Isaacs (1885–1948) has had a noticeable impact on thinking about young children and how they learn through their own explorations. Her world-famous Malting House Nursery in Cambridge gave children basic resources with which to play, to create and investigate, under minimum 'adult interference'. Isaacs' classic books, *Intellectual Growth in Young Children* (1930) and *Social*

Development in Young Children (1933), are based entirely on her observations. They show children, in her words, 'as living individuals'.

Two other famous observers need to be mentioned for their rather different techniques and viewpoints. Konrad Lorenz and Niko Tinbergen were both zoologists and their method is known as *ethology*. The ethologist sets out to catalogue behaviour as body movements and facial expressions, and to correlate observations with the stimuli that cause them. While this method has occasionally been adapted to the study of children (e.g. Blurton-Jones 1972) it has been more generally used by animal scientists. Lorenz and Tinbergen, for example, have respectively investigated geese and herring gulls in this way.

Because there is potential confusion between the concepts of ecological and ethological behaviour studies, it may be helpful to clarify them. In terms of similarity, both are concerned with observing unobtrusively, in a way that manipulates neither the environment nor the subjects. They both attempt to describe behaviour in natural settings. Where they differ is in terms of breadth. Ecologists generally focus on fairly *large* units of behaviour – for example, sand play. On the other hand ethologists focus on *smaller* units – facial expressions, gestures, body posture and eye gaze. Ecologists are more interested in the purpose and sense of the episode as a whole (as in environmental ecology), while ethologists concentrate on behaviour patterns. Ecologists are advised to describe the quality of actions (e.g. *how* things are done) whereas the ethologist would regard qualitative interpretation as unscientific.

Contemporary views of child development

The march of history can be presented to seem like a positive, cumulative progression towards a superior present-day pinnacle of understanding. With regard to everyday, taken-for-granted, general 'knowledge' about children at the beginning of the twenty-first century, it is true that there is extensive factual information available even though there are still enormous gaps as well as many conflicting opinions. One must always be ready to question the validity of knowledge. It may prove to be less coherent and objective, less securely based, than it seems at first. In the previous section we traced the history of the observational study of children. We saw that some of these studies led to the construction of theories about development. In evaluating these and any other theories it is critically important to investigate the circumstances that led to the gen-

eration of the theory in the first place. When was the research carried out? What was the nature and size of the sample on which the theory was based? What kinds of hypotheses were already in the mind of the researcher? What kind of 'mindset' did he (usually, until recently, he) have as he set about interpreting the data? These are some of the questions to be asked. In this section four important theoretical perspectives on child development will be examined: developmental 'norms', attachment, cognitive development, and the cultural and ecological view of development.

Developmental 'norms'

Developmental 'norms' are the sequential steps through which all children can be expected to progress. Typically these are considered under headings such as physical, cognitive, and social and emotional development (though some would add other categories, for instance, communication and moral development). Within each category the stages of development are usually presented in hierarchical form starting with the simplest, and these stages are usually linked to children's ages. We may well ask where these norms have come from. Their primary source is the work of American psychologists, especially Arnold Gesell, during the first half of the twentieth century. Through observations of children, often in laboratory settings, and through the collection of data, they created a structure which has formed the basis for the assessment of children ever since. Developmental norms are referred to not only by professionals. Parents too draw on them to judge their children's progress. The same norms are also used the world over; they are not restricted to their country of origin.

It is disconcerting to ponder the sources of this profoundly influential work. The researchers were almost without exception male, white, middle-class psychologists. Their research aim was to identify the universal, normal stages of development through which *all* children pass. Their actual subjects, though, were virtually all white and living in the relatively prosperous USA of the twentieth century. Information was gathered in the special child study centres attached to universities (and indeed information continues to be gathered in the 'clinical' setting of university laboratories). Ben Bradley's criticisms bring the issue sharply into focus:

> Much experimental work on infancy takes place *in vitro* – on the social equivalent of a desert island... there is no way for most studies to

represent the different anxieties, responsibilities, standards of living, demands of other children, interpersonal relationships and work commitments which shape the lives of parents, and hence of their children. Many studies focus only on well-educated, middle-class mothers with small families. (Bradley 1989, p.155)

The same critic also reminds us how far these settings are from the reality of life for many. It is after all estimated that a large and growing percentage of the world's population live in poverty. Disease and starvation are rife. 'Domestic violence continues, marriages break up, wars rage on, prescriptions for tranquillisers and stress-related diseases run at record levels.' (Bradley 1989, p.157).

Mary Sheridan's *Children's Developmental Progress* (1973) is an example of the way an influential handbook can shape thinking for decades. As a medical doctor, Sheridan selected for her framework what she termed 'the four outstanding human *biological* achievements' [my italics] (p.4) – Posture and Large Movements, Vision and Fine Movements, Hearing and Speech, and Social Behaviour and Play. Readers will note that there is no separate category for cognitive development. For each of these areas she developed her 'Stycar sequences' based on observations and photographs of the children with whom she came into contact during the 1950s. Her book, first published in 1960, has been updated and is still in print. The general acceptance and very widespread use of the Sheridan guidelines for all children, no matter how extraordinarily different their situation, is at last being challenged. Comparative studies of the very different cultural styles of caring for young children worldwide have sharpened awareness of the sheer variety and flexibility of human development. Scepticism has also been voiced about the dangerous effects of prescriptive guidelines or checklists on parents. The checklist mentality can result in parental anxieties, competitive attitudes, over- or under-expectation, and rigidity of thinking about children's progress. More recently the many subtle effects of gender difference in child development have also become clearer. Furthermore, the assessment of children with disabilities all too often relies on the use of scales of so-called 'normal' development, making it difficult to strike a balance between identifying where help is needed for some special need while still valuing the positive, unproblematic aspects of the child's development. The rich and unique individuality of every growing person can easily be devalued by over-concentration on measurement and the achievement of norms.

Until comparatively recently few texts on child development considered the implications of our multicultural society and an anti-racist stance. It is true that the Working Group Against Racism in Children's Resources (WGARCR) did set up a working group on the topic and produced a study of textbooks, *Guidelines for the Selection and Evaluation of Child Development Books* (1991). Their publication helped the reader to recognise the values and assumptions that underlie and reinforce racism; to be conscious of the transmission of blatant or subtle racist messages; to value diversity of child-rearing practices; and to question the usefulness of certain texts on child development. Very few texts were found to be written from an anti-racist, multicultural and multilingual point of view. Indeed the literature barely acknowledged any form of discrimination at all whether in terms of social class, disability, gender difference or sexual orientation.

Attachment

The way that adults perceive children and the experiences children receive through their parents may well be influenced by their sense of 'attachment'. One definition of 'attachment' is the close, continuous relationship with at least one other person that human beings need in order to develop a confident, stable, integrated personality. Attachment theory is predominantly associated with the name of John Bowlby (1907–1980), a British psychiatrist. The circumstances leading to the creation of the theory are a telling example of the significance of knowing the context. After the Second World War, Bowlby was commissioned by the World Health Organisation to investigate the plight of children who had been orphaned or separated from their parents as a consequence of the devastating conflict in Europe. These children were all in some kind of care – with foster parents or in institutions. From his research and reflections he concluded that without an intense, close relationship with a mother in the first three years a child was doomed, since 'mother love in infancy and childhood is as important for mental health as are vitamins and protein for physical health' (1951, p.158). He later (1969) went so far as to say that almost any psychiatric disorder can be linked to an impaired capacity for bonding and that such disorders in later life are frequently the result of some disturbance in bonding in early childhood. He believed that certain conditions were absolutely essential. The child must have a loving relationship with one particular person (usually the mother); the resulting attachment must continue unbroken for the first three years; it should ideally be centred within the child's own family and offer adequate stimulation. In the 2000s it is hard to grasp the powerful impact of Bowlby's publications some 50 years ago. Politicians at the time found his thesis useful in validating their decisions to close day nurseries and encourage women back into the home. There were strong social pressures persuading women to care for their children 24 hours a day (even if this was not exactly what Bowlby had said) and feeling that to do otherwise would be damaging. Bowlby's studies left out any consideration of the more communal shared care of children that is commonplace in many cultural groups. We now recognise that such shared child-rearing is very much more beneficial for the mental health of women than the rather closed, private style common in the UK where parent and child are in a 'monotropic' relationship (comparable to monogamy). Michael Rutter's important critique, *Maternal Deprivation Reassessed* (1972), and other research reports have restored the balance. If anything, the danger now is that attachment, and all that it entails, is not given the emphasis it deserves. (Chapter Five includes a section which explores attachment in relation to observations.)

Cognitive development

Jean Piaget has been introduced earlier in this chapter, and his background in biology and zoology noted. Because of his biological thinking he underlined the processes by which innate tendencies motivate the developing person to interact with the environment. Piaget was yet another white, male European whose theories have been revered the world over. His 'stage' theory of cognitive development was generated through his observations and through setting children special tasks and questioning them on what they were doing. His so-called 'clinical interviewing' has, over the years, been replicated in many countries. The special tasks were said to give insight into the different styles of thinking at successive stages of development. To give a famous example, children under six will claim, when asked, that there is more liquid in a tall thin glass than a short, squat one, even though they have seen the very same liquid poured from one glass to the other.

Piaget's work has been subjected to much scrutiny. Among the key criticisms of his ideas several stand out. First, he gave insufficient emphasis to language and social aspects. Second, his concept of egocentricity (which seems to have captured popular imagination) leads to a devaluing of the competence of small children. Third, Piagetian stage theory has had the unfortunate negative effect of restricting the thinking of some educators concerning young children. Fourth, Piaget inferred that children lack logic, disregarding the fact that, in being asked to make sense of logical problems, children are affected by the *whole context*, and in particular try to 'read' what the adults expect of them. Finally, he failed to recognise the deep significance of the *cultural* context. Indeed Piaget believed that the development of the mind was independent of its social environment. Some have portrayed the Piagetian child as a 'lonely scientist' trying to make sense of the world by her/his own efforts.

A cultural and ecological view of development

Drawing on an entirely different view of development, Lev Vygotsky (1896–1934) and his colleagues in Russia challenged the Piagetian view that the formation of the basic structures in the human mind is universally the same and not dependent on the child's cultural environment. In contrast to the perception of the child as a 'lonely scientist', Vygotsky saw a child's development as deeply embedded in a society, the child being a meaningful member of a cultural group from birth. Vygotsky's theory evolved in its own historical and geographical context. During the 1920s and 1930s (in Leninist and Stalinist times) Vygotsky travelled across the USSR observing the diverse cultural situations in which young children were being reared – from nomadic environments to relatively sophisticated urban communities, from the Siberian cold to the comparatively lush Georgian farmlands.

Vygotsky's scattered writings took time to become integrated into Western thinking and the insights derived from his work are still being developed. Nevertheless, the deep significance of the cultural group in Vygotskian theory is clear:

> in the process of development, children begin to use the same forms of behaviour in relation to themselves that others used in relation to them. Children master the social forms of behaviour and transfer these forms to themselves… Any function in the child's cultural development appears twice, or on two planes. First it appears on the social plane, and then on the psychological plane. (Wertsch 1985, p.64)

The development of language, and of adults' supporting role in children's learning, are major issues in Vygotsky's work and will be discussed later

UNIVERSITY OF WINCHESTER LIBRARY

(Chapter Five). Barbara Rogoff (1990, 2003), in her development of Vygotsky's theories, has emphasised that while all humans share a great deal of universal activity (learning to walk, speaking a language, etc.) there is nevertheless tremendous variety in styles of living. In particular, each community will have its own goals for children's development, what she calls 'valued skills'.

One other psychologist, Urie Bronfenbrenner, must be included in this chapter. His *Ecology of Human Development* (1979) similarly draws on cross-cultural comparisons of families bringing up children. His ecological philosophy widens the context for development still further to include not only the child's immediate family and cultural group but the total setting in which that community finds itself. This brings in such matters as the legal framework, economic and employment possibilities, and finally the wider beliefs, ideologies and attitudes current at that time. Bronfenbrenner gave labels to these settings or systems and compared them with the nesting arrangements of Russian dolls, successively one within another. The child (the smallest doll as it were) belongs to one or more *micro-systems* (the family, the school, the church, etc.). The interactions between the various micro-systems he called *meso-systems* (for example the relationships between family and school, family and neighbourhood). Beyond the meso-systems are the *exo-systems*, to which children do not normally have access (these include local government and the parents' workplaces). The largest outer 'Russian doll', the *macro-system*, refers to the ideological contexts – attitudes, values and beliefs generally held by the population at large. (Views on children and childhood are discussed in Chapter Two.)

CHAPTER 4

Observational Methods and Practice

Setting up an observation: recording methods

This chapter is intended to be highly practical and is designed especially to help students or practitioners make the most suitable choice of recording method for their purpose. Learning how to observe and find the words, the 'right' kind of language, to describe complex dynamic behaviour is more difficult than one might think. It is an art, almost akin to writing a short story, though this is not fiction, even if everyone is inevitably writing from within their own perspective. Furthermore, some kind of structured format is needed for the observer, rather than just approaching the task in a random and intuitive manner. But no format can be perfect and in this book attention is often drawn to some of the relative strengths and limitations of the different methods described.

Underlying issues

The first task is to clarify the reason for the observations. Student courses will almost certainly require observational studies within their professional framework. The aim may be to learn about child development, to study some single aspect of play (e.g. imaginative play), to discern relationships in context, to heighten general awareness of children's play and the way they construct meanings, or perhaps to focus on some specific process such as a child 'settling in' to a new situation. Observation within the day-to-day early years settings should ideally have functions over and above amassing records for the *Early Years Foundation Stage Profile* (EYFSP) or other assessment procedures. Possible examples would be charting different gender responses to selected activities, exploring the behaviour of a child causing concern, or investigating the different contexts in which a bilingual child uses one language or the other.

Using observation as a tool through which students can study child development has its risks. Certainly it can provide insights into 'normative development', where a single child serves as a typical example of all children of that particular age. But such an approach can narrow thinking. One child cannot of course stand for all the rest. Every child is unique, and uniqueness can be difficult to grasp (Baldwin 1994).

The frame of mind of the observer is significant too. What are her or his prior expectations in this observational task? We tend to see what we are looking for. Our observations are highly coloured by our preconceptions and mental states – for example witnesses of the same event often give conflicting accounts of what occurred. Carrying out an observation is almost like a fishing exercise using nets with different sized holes. What you catch depends not only on when and where you fish but also on your gear. In early education settings teachers will probably often have the EYFSP categories in mind as they observe. They may be trawling for suitable examples, typically written on yellow 'post-it' notes. With this kind of focus they may well overlook much more complicated behaviour indicating deep emotions or complex thought processes (see the St Stephen's case study in Chapter Ten). Mary Jane Drummond (1993) has given a medical example of the way assessment may lead to restricted observation (see Chapter Seven of this book).

When engaged in research at any level students will first need to define which aspects of a child's behaviour they want to concentrate on in order to gather data. This establishing of the frame is necessary but does bring its own consequences – are the selected aspects truly representative of the topic under investigation? Another danger, that of inappropriate context, is nicely exemplified by Woodhead and Faulkener (2000, pp9–10). As a young psychologist trying to carry out one-to-one activities with young children in a room away from the rest of the class Woodhead found them inexplicably unresponsive. The explanation came later from the headteacher: the activities had been taking place in the 'naughty room'. Children are acutely aware of the context and will always be trying to interpret the situation and the adult's motives. Normally they will do their best to give the adult the answer they think is expected. A classic book, *Young Children Learning: Talking and thinking at home and school* (Tizard and Hughes 1984), remains a powerful and fasci-

nating revelation of young children's apparent capacities in the different contexts of home and school.

Equally, children sometimes have private agendas. Susan Engel illustrates this through the case of her son's annual check-up at the paediatric clinic. Jake, her four-year-old, had recently undergone ear surgery. He was asked to draw a man – the test where the number of limbs and detail indicate the level of cognitive development. To his mother's dismay Jake's figure had no arms and legs, though the rest was there. As they stood up to go, Jake said somewhat offhandedly, 'See that man I drew? He used to have two legs and two arms, but the doctor cut them off!' (Engel 2005, p.28).

Since children keep trying to make sense of the adults' intentions, the type of recording in any observational situation must take this into account. The student will decide whether it is appropriate visibly to take notes or record or video during the observation. In social work children may be subjected to much scrutiny and become highly attuned to different case workers and their methods. Some may refuse to co-operate further and even find it difficult anyway to communicate with social workers (Turney 2008). In some situations such as observations in a child's own home where the observation concerns the parents too, note-taking would seem very intrusive (Miller *et al.* 1989).

Selecting a method

Whatever method is to be used, it will take time to become proficient and confident. Personal reflection on and evaluation of the process are vital, as is constructive discussion with colleagues, tutors or other students during the learning process. While many variations and adaptations are possible, the methods divide broadly into two groups: narrative methods and sampling methods.

Narrative methods are those which simply attempt to record a slice of life in everyday language. They may be called Naturalistic Observation or narrative/free description, and both are exemplified in the Reggio and the Tavistock methods described below. There is also the Target Child method which is more structured. Diary records, in which a more or less regular daily note is made, also belong in this group. This is the least structured of all methods. (Readers may enjoy *A Father's Diary* by Fraser Harrison 1985.)

[handwritten note: Page out of order please turn over for 51-52]

Sampling methods offer ways of making more selective observations, based either on time or events – hence their names, Time Sampling and Event Sampling. The Checklist method and Rating Scale, in which observation is restricted to watching for a pre-selected range of behaviours, are also of this type. Apart from the familiar diary record, each of these methods will be explained in detail below, giving actual examples as well as listing their strengths and limitations.

Making a start on child observation studies

There are certain general points to note about observational studies which are applicable to whichever method you decide to use.

A student observation must preserve the child's anonymity. For this reason only an initial, or a pseudonym, should be used. The child's gender and age should always be recorded. The usual practice in noting the age is to state the number of years and months separated by a colon, so that for 3 years 10 months you write 3:10. You should also note the child's home language. The time of the observation will need to be noted as well as the date, since this may indicate whether the child is fresh or tired. If the observation is one of a series then a numbering system is necessary. Each observation will be numbered in sequence. Before beginning the observation any aspects of the environment that may affect the child's behaviour should be summarised. You should note down the location, the number of adults and children present, the play opportunities for the children, and what, if anything, the children are expected to be doing at that time (e.g. sitting listening to a story, or free play). This will take a few minutes and should give the observer time to tune into a possibly quite complex atmosphere with many lively children.

1. Naturalistic Observations

This narrative method is sometimes called 'specimen description', 'written record', or 'running record'. Since it is by far the simplest method, structured only by noting the sequence of time, it may be the best one to start with. Observers must write down (on the spot) as much as they can of what they are seeing. This will normally be jotted down in ordinary longhand, though it is a good idea to adopt simple abbreviations where possible, e.g. A for any adult, LH and RH for left and right hand, and so on. The present tense is used. The only materials required are therefore paper, pen or pencil. To start with, an observation of ten

minutes may be advisable but the experience of longer periods will soon be necessary. Observation can seem quite demanding until you become accustomed to the intense concentration required.

Some researchers have modified this method by using a tape-recorder in place of a note-pad. They quietly dictate their description into the microphone, transcribing the recording at a later stage. Alternatively tape-recordings of children's actual conversations can be made. These can capture the immediacy and detail of children's conversation. Blind students in particular have employed the technique with success, by taping children's play in relatively small rooms. They could then re-run the tape at home and analyse it in detail. Students should note, however, that in a lively preschool environment, possibly in a large echoing hall, good sound quality is not always easy to achieve.

Naturalistic Observation: example	
Date: 18/2/08	
Child's initial: D	Gender: M
Age: 2:8	Date of Birth: 13.6.05
Child's home language:	English
Setting:	Nursery, free play – water tray, play dough, jigsaw puzzles, children's books.
Number and age of children:	14 (2–4-year-olds)
Number of adults:	4
Activity:	Adults tidying up and encouraging children to go and sit on carpet for a story.

TIME	
9.35	D 'spooning' water with small cup into saucepan. Bending over water tray, his bottom slightly stuck out, seems slightly awkward.
9.36	A 'Go and sit on the carpet'. D keeps on water play.
9.37	A (in firm voice) 'Come and sit down D'. D, pulling up trousers, walks slowly over and sits down quietly with other children. A starts to read story. D looks at me.
9.38	D sits very still, doesn't move though he can't see the pictures properly.
9.39	Hunches up shoulders, continues to sit very still, seems to be listening very carefully.
9.40	At sight of picture of plate of biscuits says 'Bistets'. Then 'The cat wants a bistet'. A acknowledges D with 'Yes, D, the cat wants a biscuit'.

Page out of order Please turn back for 53 - 54

ADVANTAGES

- requires no advance preparation other than pen and paper
- feels 'natural' (easy to get started)
- picks up everything without selection (at least in theory)
- conveys an all-round picture of the child and the complexity of behaviour
- records the 'ecology' of the environment.

LIMITATIONS

- creates dilemmas as to what and how much to record
- produces a mass of unstructured data
- lumps all kinds of information together
- makes it difficult to compare observations.

2. The Reggio approach to observation

A short introduction to the philosophy and practice of the Reggio preschools is given in Chapter Nine. In this approach the focus is on children's learning processes. (The 5x5x5 project, described in Chapter Nine, takes a similar approach to observation and documentation, summed up in the phrase 'researching children researching the world'). Children are seen as members of learning groups building a 'collective body of knowledge'. Listening is not only the source of understanding but a key element. Reggio educators talk of a 'pedagogy of listening' (Giudici, Rinaldi and Krechevsky 2001). Teachers and educators are not like video recorders. Their note-taking assumes choices and interpretations.

The actual recording method in Reggio takes special care to incorporate the interactions among several children. Often they use a large sheet of paper with a separate column for each child and each adult. In order to see the sequence of the dialogue, the contributions are successively numbered. Other forms of record-keeping then complement the written notes, notably photographic and video images, and the children's drawings, plans and models. The aim is to gather any relevant fragments or traces of the current project.

Reggio documentation: Example (translated notes typed up after a session extracted from Giudici *et al.* 2000, p.106)					
Caterina	Luca	Ferruccio	Laura	Isabella	[teacher notes]
2. Nice!	1. Lodi did this one… It looks like a fish. 4. (talking to himself) Here's a ladder…	6. We put a man here, sitting on the bridge, a leg came from this hole…		3. Ferro, Luca, Caterina, Martina… 5. Do you remember what we did? 7. Apart from that, let's take a look… There were our two trees…the big tree…	
	8. It's our little itsy bitsy…				

ADVANTAGES

- has the same advantages as the narrative method
- brings together the interactions between children and adults
- displays traces of the ideas more easily
- lets children observe the documentation process
- helps children learn about other children's thinking as well as their own
- teaches children the processes of enquiry. (For example a child said to an artist: 'Write this down, Kath, this is important.')

LIMITATIONS

- resembles those of narrative method recording

- requires more practice and involves more writing in the Reggio approach

- takes time and experience to become confident about what to focus on and to select for recording.

3. Target Child method

The origins of this style of recording can be traced back to the methods used in the study of animals by ethologists (see Chapter Three). The actual Target Child method was developed by Kathy Sylva and her colleagues during the 1970s as a tool for investigating preschool children's behaviour, in particular for studying children's powers of concentration and the circumstances that promote this. That study was part of the Oxford Preschool Research Project and has continued to be used by both students and practitioners in varied situations. Basically it is a straightforward technique using a simple pre-coding system for collecting data. A little advance preparation is required in the form of drawing up a grid on which to record the observation, and for deciding on suitable abbreviations. A full description can be found in Sylva, Roy and Painter (1980, Appendix A), but the essential information needed to use the method can be found below.

The completed recording is shown in Figure 4.1. A watch, ideally one showing seconds, will be required so that you can record minute by minute both the activity and the language used. Each number on the sheet represents one minute. The abbreviations suggested will help to speed up note-taking, but of course you can create your own.

TC = target child (the one you are observing)

C   = any other child

A   = any adult (a member of staff, a parent helper, another student, or you)

>   = speaks to

In the activity record column you write down *what the child does* within each minute period, while in the language record column you record verbatim *everything the child says*. You can also add conversation directed towards the target child in the language column, e.g. A > TC 'Come and have your drink' or 'I wonder if…'. The other two columns are normally used once the observation is completed. The first (labelled task) is based

on the actual task the child engaged in – e.g. painting, music – which may be noted using letter codes. (This coding is useful if the purpose of the observation is to study specific preschool activities. Task coding is set out in the Appendix.) The final column (labelled social) affords an opportunity to pick out from the record the types of social contacts the child was engaging in, whether playing alone, in parallel, in a small or large group. Twenty minutes is a suitable length of time to observe, though you may like to start with ten minutes and build up to the longer time span. Do not worry if you are interrupted for any reason. Simply write 'Interruption' and resume as soon as you can. (See Chapter Five for ways to analyse the Target Child observation.)

Date: 1.3.95 Time: 10.01 Child's Initial: P Gender: M			
Age: 2:8 Date of Birth: 13.6.92			
Setting: Nursery, free play (jigsaws, dressing-up, painting, etc.). 8 children, 2 adults. One A with large cardboard boxes, tubes and big cardboard cable reels (like wheels)			
Activity Record	**Language Record**	**Task**	**Social**
1. P picks up tube in RH. Bashes cardboard reel with it	C > P, You're breaking it. A > C, No, he's not. Those are for making it. P makes whacking noises		
2. Stands very still, watching other children and listening. Almost in a dream-like state	A explains about making a caravan for children to sit in, using boxes and spools		
3. Watches A and three children arranging boxes and wheels for the caravan. Hands on hips	A > P, What could that bit be for P? P, I don't know		
4. Watching closely, kneels down. Puts tube in box. Takes it out. A gives P end of strong, wide sellotape	A > P, Can you help me? A > P, Will you hold that? Can you pull on this?		
5. Starts to pull tape, it's too hard for him. Grits teeth, look of determination	A > P, Keep on pulling P A (explains how they are making caravan)		
6. Pushes roll of tape back along top of box (A guides him). Other children push and shove around	A > P, Where does it go this time? P, That way? A > P, Let someone else have a go		

7. Walks slowly away. Looks at jigsaw table and children there. Wanders to alphabet chart on wall			
8. Returns to group making caravan. Picks up one reel, takes it away, and then another, making a pile away from the construction	A > P, Can you bring them over here?		
9. Puts reels one by one in big box (caravan). Carries last one to boy lying down	P, There's a wheel for you C, Thank you		
10. Wanders back to caravan construction. Takes another wheel to lying down boy, smiling broadly	Laughs with funny squeaky gleeful sound		
11.			
12.			

ADVANTAGES

- needs only basic preparation of grid
- focuses observation by use of simple grid structure, which also aids later analysis
- is flexible and open-ended.

LIMITATIONS

- takes a little practice to become proficient with the method
- requires some preparation
- constrains some observers by imposing a grid structure.

4. The Tavistock approach

Since 1948 a distinctive model of infant observation has been central to the training of child psychotherapists, originating at the Tavistock Clinic in London and subsequently adopted for other courses. In the original model the Tavistock approach concentrated on the development of babies (from soon after birth) in the family home. The experience of this

form of observation should assist students to understand and manage their own emotions as well as coming to terms with the dynamics of the family situation under observation. Margaret Rustin, one of the leading psychotherapists at the Tavistock, wrote, 'the practice of systematic observation of the development of infants provides the observer with an opportunity to encounter primitive emotional states in the infant and his family, and indeed the observer's own response to this turbulent environment' (Rustin 1989, p.7).

According to this method the observer makes hour-long observations every week for two years. Students do not take notes in the presence of the family but make a detailed record *after* the visit, describing in as much detail as possible what they have witnessed. The observations are recorded in 'literal, everyday, untheorised language' (Rustin 1989, p.74). The students attend weekly seminars (in small groups, typically of five members) at which they present, in turn, observations of the babies. At the heart of the Tavistock approach is psychoanalytical theory which accepts the need to pay attention to the emotional impact on the observer in addition to the observed child's feelings. 'Emotion holds a cardinal place; it has to be observed and recorded and it will occur in the observer and the reader. It is not a distraction or a contaminant. Correctly grasped, the emotional factor is an indispensable tool to be used in the service of greater understanding' (Miller 1989, p.3).

Tavistock Method: example

A short description of the family introduces the chapter:

'Andrew is the second of two children; his older brother was two and a half when he was born. His parents, both in their early thirties, are a well-educated, middle-class couple…'

Observation at 3 weeks

At the first observation, mother had much to say after our initial exchanges: 'Luckily he sleeps a lot, even at night; my first child was always awake during the night. It was terrible! At the moment he is not sleeping really deeply because of his cold; I have a cold too. Sometimes the baby seems old and tired, and so bored!' With a voice full of concern she continued, 'Sometimes I put him on my bed so that he has something more to look at,' and later, 'This baby is luckier than the other because now, with the other child around, there is always noise in the house. His brother often puts his face very, very near to the baby's face, smiling at him. That is wonderful for the baby, and adults never do that.'

(Miller *et al.* p.118)

ADVANTAGES

- requires no note-taking during the observation
- uses everyday language
- creates a detailed picture of the child
- includes adult interaction
- may allow for developmental changes to be seen over a long period of observation (if used in its original form)
- allows for recording adult feelings
- can enable the observer to become totally immersed.

LIMITATIONS

- demands very detailed and accurate recollection *after* the visits
- depends on considerable commitment
- can have a very powerful impact on the observer
- demands reflective discussions following observations
- risks the subconscious construction of events that did not happen
- increases concern that very close observation may seem like an invasion of privacy.

More recently the Tavistock approach has been modified to meet other circumstances. With social workers or students on higher degrees studying babies and children in care settings, another version, described below, will be preferred. In these courses the observers record their own feelings and the children's behaviour, just as they would when using the original Tavistock approach, but with various modifications. Peter Elfer (in Abbott and Langston 2005, p.121) explains his particular version as follows:

- the number of observational visits is reduced to fit the time available
- the observation period is reduced to between 20 minutes and an hour
- the student observes without a notebook and is receptive as possible to the smallest details as well as to the emotional atmosphere and responses

- after the observation it is written up in as free-flowing a way as possible giving the main sequence of events and recording as much detail as possible
- the write-up is shared with the supervisor and student colleagues and is discussed, noting differing interpretations and connections.

The synopsis of an MA student on Elfer's course usefully summarises her intent:

> The focus is on the opportunities for celebrating the experiences of the babies and infants in a toddler and carer group. These did not have to be achievements, they could be discoveries, attempts that succeeded and those that failed. They could be social experiences and personal ones, emotional and creative and I was particularly interested in how children's independence was encouraged and celebrated (Elfer 2005, p.123).

5. Time Sampling

The observational methods so far described all involve a narrative, 'story-telling' style. They give a picture of the child's behaviour in context and in enough detail to understand what was taking place. Moreover, the original order of the events is maintained. On the other hand, recording in a narrative fashion creates large amounts of data which may be difficult to analyse.

Time Sampling provides a way of recording that concentrates on one selected aspect of behaviour in order to discover its frequency patterns. As a method it originated in the United States during the 1920s for the purpose of studying children in the laboratory nursery schools then being established. The 'nervous habits' of normal children were the topic of the first time-sampling study, but the best-known was Mildred Parten's study of children's play in 1933. Time Sampling is suited only to behaviour that can actually be observed (day dreaming as a topic is therefore out) and that can be described in clear terms. The behaviour patterns must occur reasonably frequently (at least every 15 minutes) so that they can be recorded in a relatively short period of time.

The purpose of such a study must first be thoroughly worked out. If, for example, the aim is to examine the tactics by which a child obtains adult attention, then preliminary observations will be necessary in order to identify the range of possible behaviours. These behaviours in effect are markers, or indicators of the topic for investigation. In the case of a child seeking attention, the selected tactics may be verbal, such as calling out or asking politely for help, or non-verbal, such as tugging or pulling the adult. Or they may be indirect, such as disturbing other children with the same purpose of attracting attention. These behaviours must be detailed precisely so that they can easily be identified during the observation session. In practice this means devising a kind of checklist (further discussed in the section on the Checklist method later in this chapter).

Time Sampling: example
TOPIC: Getting adult attention

The playgroup leader is concerned about M, a boy aged 3:6. She believes that he is making excessive demands on the adults, and wishes to find out how frequently this really is happening and what types of behaviour he is using. Having identified the range of strategies he tends to use, she has grouped them as follows:

Verbal attention-seeking: *acceptable* forms include:
'Please may I...?, 'I'd like..., or addresses the adult by name.

Verbal attention-seeking: *undesirable* forms include:
'Give me...' (in very demanding tones), swearing, screaming and shouting out very loudly.

Non-verbal attention-seeking: *acceptable* forms includes:
taps or pats adult, looks into her face and stands right in front of her.

Non-verbal attention-seeking: *undesirable* forms includes:
pulling the adult roughly by her arm or clothes, pushing or punching her.

Plan for observation

The adult decides to watch for one minute at 15-minute intervals and to record the observations by ticking in the appropriate column.

Date:	Time: 9.00am	Child:			
Gender:	Age:	Home language:			
Activity:					

Language and Behaviour				Time		
		9.15	9.30	9.45	10.00	etc.
Verbal:	acceptable					
	undesirable					
Non-verbal:	acceptable					
	undesirable					

Another kind of time sampling might also be tried. In this case it is *total* behaviour, not *selected* behaviour, that is under investigation. It is a useful technique for discovering just what a child normally does throughout a day, or what kinds of social contacts she/he regularly has. For this technique the timing needs to be planned in three ways: first by deciding the total amount of time available; next the length of the time unit for observation and finally the intervals between the observational units. So, for instance, in one morning a child might be observed for one minute every fifteen minutes. The observer would note down in the one-minute observation period the child's activity (where she is and what she is doing), what she is saying, and who she is with.

Among other uses of Time Sampling is investigating some activity (such as visits to the book corner) by making notes for a minute at a pre-arranged frequency (perhaps at 30-minute intervals) which children are in the activity area and what they are doing. The temptation, of course, is to go on watching beyond the defined minute (or whatever time unit has been selected) particularly if something interesting is happening. This must be resisted.

Time Sampling: example 2
TOPIC: Study of book corner

Books have regularly been found scattered around the room at the end of the morning session. None of the adults is sure how this has happened.

Plan of observation

Every 15 minutes the observer will briefly note down the names of children in the area of the book corner, and what they are doing there.

Date: Starting Time: 9.00am

Activity: Book corner

Time	Children	What is happening
9.00	Kim and Ross	Gathering books into piles on carpet, laughing and chattering.
9.15	Raj	Sitting quietly, looking at pictures in alphabet book.
9.30	Kim and Ross	Trying to climb on book-shelves, giggling.
9.45	Kim, Ross and Winston	Replacing a few books on the shelves, Winston telling the others what to do.
etc.		

ADVANTAGES

- gathers precise, focused information
- collects a large amount of data in a relatively short period
- records information that is easily understood
- allows the fine grain of a particular behaviour to be studied
- allows comparisons to be made (e.g. of children of different ages)
- may reveal unsuspected patterns of behaviour.

LIMITATIONS

- demands accurate time-keeping (possibly over a whole morning)
- collects fragmentary information
- merely samples behaviour, which may be unrepresentative
- studies only overt and frequent behaviours
- is unsuitable for investigating such topics as imaginative play
- does not reveal why certain behaviours occur
- fails to examine the quality of experiences
- pre-determines observation, so risking bias and potential neglect of important behaviour.

6. Event Sampling

The perennial problem with all observation is how to deal with large quantities of data generated by the complex activity that has been observed. Whereas *time* sampling, as we have seen, selects data from the stream of events, *event* sampling selects by concentrating on a particular short period of behaviour. It is helpful in investigating such episodes as quarrels, say, or in looking at a child's problem-solving behaviour within a defined period. Other suitable topics for event sampling might be tidying-up sessions, observing a small group on an outing, or an activity like listening to a story. The unit of observation is the event itself, which may be of any length. While it is unwise to attempt to observe for too long a period, the actual observation time cannot be decided in advance. In preparation it is necessary to identify clearly the topic you are interested in and exactly what information you are after. In the case of a quarrel, you may want to know how long it lasted, what was happening before it began, who was involved, what he or she said and did, what brought the quarrel to a conclusion, and what the outcome was. With this technique it is usual to recommend the preparation of a recording sheet in advance so that you can jot down information rapidly, but you will also need space for a narrative description, just as with the naturalistic description method outlined earlier. The moment to start systematic observation is when you see the event begin. You note the time and then continue to watch until the episode ends.

Event Sampling: example TOPIC: Frequency and type of play between D and W		
D is new in the group and still unsure of himself. Often he seems to be playing with W (a year older) who is very excitable (perhaps even hyperactive). Staff feel that D is getting into trouble because of W's leadership.		
Date: 07.02.05 Starting Time: 9.00 Activity: Free play Ages: D 2:8 W 3:10		
Number	Time and Length	Event
1.	9.15 (1 minute)	W > D 'Let's play picnics'. They rush into home corner, grabbing bags and pretend food. Take it to the climbing frame. D drops everything he is carrying and joins adult at craft table.
2.	9.45 (5 minutes)	D joins W at climbing frame saying, 'There's a fire' W shouts, 'Get everything out!' They throw everything out (they had collected clothes, jigsaws, etc.). A 'Calm down, let's put it all away.' W and D lie down inside the climbing frame and refuse to come out, etc.

ADVANTAGES

- suits any reasonably short, defined event

- helps in defining and understanding particular situations

- aids later analysis since the 'event' itself forms the structure.

LIMITATIONS

- requires an alert, available observer to pick up the cue of an imminent event

- produces data lacking the clarity of Time Sampling

UNIVERSITY OF WINCHESTER LIBRARY

- may lead to less objective observation since behaviours are predefined.

7. Checklist method

The checklist is a very familiar tool, for shopping, jobs to be done, and so on. In the context of observation it is simply a list of behaviours deemed to be important, which can be ticked off as and when they are noted. Checklists are commonly used for recording stages of development in health, education and other areas, but they cannot of course take the place of observation – they are better thought of as summaries of observations. The 'standards' of the *Early Years Foundation Stage Profile* might in effect be termed checklists.

In the section on Time Sampling above a checklist of a sort has been described where the items were linked to frequency of occurrence. The preparation for the Checklist method obviously includes the preliminary creation of an actual list. Target behaviours have to be selected, defined precisely, and the list organised logically (typically from the simple to the more complex). Two types of checklist are given as examples below, a simple checklist and a rating scale.

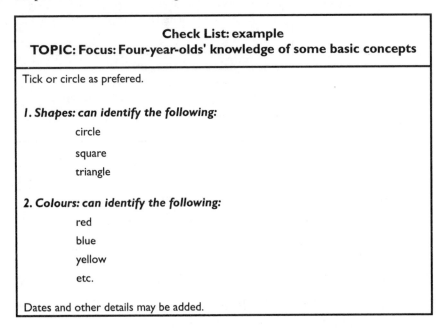

Check List: example
TOPIC: Focus: Four-year-olds' knowledge of some basic concepts

Tick or circle as prefered.

1. Shapes: can identify the following:

circle

square

triangle

2. Colours: can identify the following:

red

blue

yellow

etc.

Dates and other details may be added.

A Rating Scale is another kind of checklist where an aspect of behaviour is considered and then judged, or 'rated', for entry at some point on a scale. A five-point scale is very commonly adopted. The advantage of the Rating Scale over the basic checklist is that it grades the level of response rather than confining it to a simple yes or no. The data can then be transferred easily to a computer spreadsheet.

Rating Scale: example
TOPIC: Co-operation

Tick the statement most closely corresponding to the observed behaviour.

1. Very keen to work/play with others

2. Seems to like working/playing with others

3. Works/plays satisfactorily

4. Mostly works/plays alone

5. Never works/plays with others.

ADVANTAGES

- is simple to use, once the list is constructed
- uses the observer's time efficiently
- produces records that are easy to read and understand
- shows immediately what a child can and cannot do
- notes behaviours as soon as they occur
- assists making comparisons e.g. of age or gender.

LIMITATIONS

- depends entirely on the soundness of the checklist
- may include trivia because they are easy to observe and 'tick off'
- gives no information about quality of behaviour
- does not reveal reasons for behaviour
- poses risk of observer subjectivity creating biased results.

Setting up an observation: contacting a preschool group and selecting a child

The circumstances in which observations are carried out vary widely and this book attempts to offer guidance across many possible situations. Whoever works with young children as part of their day-to-day responsibilities will have their own reasons for undertaking observations, some of which have already been mentioned. Students on a course are, by contrast, in a very different position and may first have to find children to study. Most of this section addresses the needs of students rather than staff in their everyday workplace.

If as a student you need a preschool placement it is obviously a good idea to seek out, if possible, some setting within easy reach in your own locality. There are many early years settings going under various names, such as parent-and-toddler groups, crèches, preschools, nurseries and children's centres. Opening times may vary but now, with good websites available, it is easy enough to find basic information. As a general rule it is better to observe in a setting open to all children rather than one confined to children attending primarily for therapeutic reasons. Most settings should now in fact include a cross-section of children. (See Chapter Six for details of English early years services.)

Among the first things to check is whether the setting has students already, perhaps like you engaged on observations, and whether it can still comfortably accommodate you. A letter of introduction, explaining the purpose of the observation task and what is expected of the setting, should already have been issued to the student ready to hand to the person in charge. Most settings are remarkably generous with their hospitality towards students, recognising that this is a vital part of the process of learning about children.

Setting up an observation offers a valuable experience in communication. The letter of introduction is only the preliminary to a fuller explanation of the observation project. It is essential to acquaint the staff with such details as the number of visits the student intends, their timing and duration, and their purpose. Finally, it is important to reassure everyone working in the setting that the observations will not be in any way judgmental or reflect critically on the setting itself. The object is solely to facilitate student learning. Confidentiality will be maintained throughout, all participants being treated in the observation record as anonymous and unidentifiable. The request to observe will clearly be made in such a way that the setting could easily refuse. Furthermore, you must seek prior permission from the child's parent(s) or guardian(s), who should have a perfect right to turn down the proposal without loss of face. Preschool staff are usually helpful in assisting contact between the parents and the student. Gaining a child's agreement to observational studies will be dealt with below.

Being present as an observer raises several significant issues. Students will not wish to be too conspicuous as a visitor to avoid attracting unnecessary attention and so affecting the interactions. More importantly, it is wise for the student observer to take into account his or her own gender, class and race in relation to the majority of the staff, parents and children. Thus a white male student in a largely female, ethnically mixed group will inevitably have a different impact from that of a black female student in the same setting. However well-meaning, self-effacing and anti-racist we believe ourselves to be, we may still appear to others as prejudiced through our class, the language we use and our personal style. It is notoriously difficult to empathise fully with other people's life experiences for we cannot get inside another person's skin. Disability and gender bring up some of the same issues as race. It is to be hoped that course programmes will give students ample opportunity for in-depth study of all such anti-discriminatory matters. The topic is raised here because you may not realise the kind of power you exercise as a seemingly humble student observer. In your choice of which child to study you must avoid letting stereotyping and prejudice hamper your objectivity, especially if you select a child from a culture other than your own. Equally there are risks in choosing a child whom you assume to be very much of your own class and culture (perhaps even imagining this child somehow to resemble your younger self). The importance of an open mind cannot be emphasised too strongly. Students who are also parents are advised to select a child of a different age from their own, if at all possible, so that they do not dwell overmuch on comparisons.

Children's consent

A significant step in setting up an observation involves getting the child's permission. There is no question that respecting the child's rights in this matter should be of first importance. Article 12 of the UN Convention on the Rights of the Child (1989) states the right of the child to be consulted. In the past, children's competence to give consent has been seriously underestimated. Children should, however, be 'authentic contributors and decision makers in meaningful classroom pedagogy...' and should likewise agree to any processes that affect them (Harcourt and Conroy 2005, p.568). Harcourt and Conroy list various matters children should be aware of:

- the nature of the research
- exactly what will be expected of them
- any possible risks of the research
- their right to withdraw at any time
- what will happen to collected data and possible audiences for the research
- the fact that they must not be pressured by any inducements
- the fact that all forms of consent must be documented and approved *prior* to data collecting.

(Harcourt and Conroy 2005, p.569)

How all this is explained to the child will depend on her/his age and ability to comprehend but it is in fact a good learning opportunity in communication. Finding the language to put this request to a young child may require thought beforehand, especially for a student unfamiliar with that age-group. Remember that children, like adults, must feel they have a genuine chance to say no.

Carrying out an observation

The role of observer needs careful consideration since it is likely to be different from any other roles the student is familiar with. In some ways it may feel unnaturally passive, despite being quite mentally demanding. New observers indeed often find the intense concentration required fairly tiring. Your job, whatever the form of recording chosen, is to absorb and note down as much of the behaviour of your focus child as you can. You are there to take in information, not to respond or to act. This is best achieved by staying as unobtrusive as possible, endeavouring to make your physical movements quiet and undemonstrative, so as not to attract attention. If convenient, sit near the action. If you have to stand, maintain an attentive stillness. You will have come prepared with recording sheets or notebook, and perhaps a watch, but it is best to delay for at least ten minutes before starting the observation. Use this adjustment period to absorb the atmosphere and to start making sense of a potentially very lively scene. Meanwhile you can be noting down the basic facts about the scene, the number of adults and children, the available materials, and the structure of activities in progress. When you are ready to begin the observation, give the task your entire attention. Sometimes it is hard to avoid being side-tracked, perhaps by another child, but be as self-disciplined as you can.

Some common problems

When adults in preschool settings are unused to student observers they may need help in understanding what is involved. In the first place, as an observer you will prefer an ordinary, everyday session in which no special arrangements have been made either for you or for the child being observed. You want everyone to continue as normal, as if no observer were present. Second, the purpose of your visit is merely to observe, not to assist or to look after the children if someone happens to be called away. Nor is this a social visit – so the observer must avoid being drawn into general conversation. Students may be surprised to find themselves being put into the role of expert and asked for advice. All these dilemmas can be dealt with in a friendly but firm way. Much more worrying is handling a situation that causes you, as onlooker, personal concern. Perhaps you feel that children are not being treated with respect, or you may overhear racist or sexist remarks. It is difficult to give general advice here, but as a visitor with a specific role – solely that of observer – you should intervene only if you perceive immediate physical danger. Your position is that of the 'good citizen'. When you do have unresolved anxieties then raise them with your course tutor or possibly (while continuing to ensure anonymity) discuss them in a course seminar.

Yet another scenario may present itself. The child you are observing, or another child in the setting, tries to interrupt you. They may be curious. They may ask what you are doing (even if they have given their consent), sometimes trying to tempt their observer into a game by making enticing remarks, such as 'Does this tiger go in this hole? Oh no, he doesn't, that one's for the lion!' Some may make even stronger attempts to capture your interest. Such curiosity is normal, natural behaviour. Young children depend on interaction with the more experienced members of their community and this includes people like you. They have an insatiable appetite for involvement and conversation with adults. During an observation session what should you do? In a calm friendly way just get on with your task. Should they ask 'What are you doing?', answer honestly: 'I'm writing about the children's play.' As already mentioned, you may become aware of the risk of an accident occurring, a situation in which a child could possibly be hurt and which no other adult seems to have noticed. Only then might you justifiably, and sensibly, step in.

Observation in a home setting

Some courses require students to make one or more home visits as part of their child study. Observation in a private home is bound to be different from a group setting with perhaps 20 or more children and several adults. The observer is now without doubt in a very different relationship with both child(ren) and adult(s). Greater empathy and respect will be needed, for this is not a public, community facility, but a private and very personal world. You might, as an observer, feel that this is an intrusive activity and even that it is not appropriate. Visits to homes by students on child observation courses can be viewed in another way though, and those tutors and organisations with experience of home-visiting back this up in their research findings. Most parents truly welcome genuine interest in their child and her or his development. Given the chance, the majority of parents will talk freely, and with pleasure, about their child's history and interests. British society is not always tolerant of parents who boast publicly of their child's achievements, which may explain why it is usually easy to engage parents in purely private conversation about their offspring. The essential points to convey to parents are that the child being studied is fully respected and valued, and that the student appreciates the insights and information gained from interviewing the parents and observing the child. Every child is unique and every study built up in this way is similarly unique.

Conclusion of a series of observational visits

As you near the end of the series of visits it is worth giving some thought as to how you wish to conclude them. This applies even to a relatively short observation programme. Apart from your more obvious duties, such as expressing thanks and ensuring your hosts know that this will be your final day with them, it should also be an opportunity to confirm they understand what you intend doing with all those notes you have been diligently taking. The observations belong to the student. They are purely study materials and there is no obligation to show them either to the parents or to staff.

Evaluation of observational visits

For the sake of clarity, reflection and analysis of observations are considered in the next chapter. There you will find suggestions about themes to explore and ways of representing and sharing your findings. The section that now follows offers some ideas about how to evaluate the process of observation itself. For a series of observational visits to become more than simply a means of gathering information, indeed for the process to be truly a learning experience, it is necessary to reflect subsequently on what occurred in a thoughtful, critical way. Observation will continue to be an important tool for you, and at this stage it is worth going beyond the obvious mechanics of what happens during observation to consider the more subtle, hidden processes at work. Schön (1987) examines the value of reflection for all professionals throughout their careers. Ideally you should have the opportunity for discussion in small seminar groups with fellow student observers as well as with tutors. Discussions with other students, comparisons of individual observations, and sharing opinions ought to benefit everyone. A group can also provide sympathetic support if this is needed. (Chapter Eight of this book discusses further the role of the seminar group on a course.)

Despite all your foresight and planning it is likely that your observational visits will have raised some practical points. Even if you feel the visits have been successful, some consideration of the reason for this is in order. Students undertaking observations as part of a course programme will in any case almost certainly be asked to evaluate the process. The following section may aid in structuring your evaluation. But first, what should be evaluated? There are two broad areas: the actual process and technique of observing, and the impact of the observations on all the people involved.

The process and technique of observation

How did you manage? What did you find difficult? Was it hard to capture *all* the action and talk? Could you write fast enough? Did your notes make sense afterwards? One likely reason for possible dissatisfaction with your actual recording technique is simply that you need more time to become proficient. As with any skill, regular practice makes all the difference. Course programmes may be overfull, and important topics like observation skills practice and reflection may not be allocated the time they deserve. You should certainly monitor your own progress and compare your abilities on your first observation visit with later. Are you becoming quicker and more fluent in recording? If you do feel inadequate at recording at first, rest assured that you will speed up in time and find the words coming more easily. One vital skill, which only improves with practice, is the ability to select what is significant. Not everything can be written down.

At the start you should have made a careful choice of which recording technique to employ. Now, after the observations, is the time to consider whether it was appropriate for your task, how well it worked and whether it should be modified in a future occasion. These methods are not set in stone and are always being adapted by researchers and practitioners to suit circumstances.

The effect on the individuals involved: the child

You need to consider what effect your presence had on the child you were observing. You should ponder how the play and group dynamics might have been altered because of your presence. The smaller the group, the stronger your possible impact might be. This is not to suggest that you should have had *no* effect, but to alert you to the fact that any visitor (especially one coming for several weeks) does make a difference, and that the difference is most often positive. Children in their preschool years learn at a particularly dramatic rate; they are inquisitive about *everything*. They seek out new experiences and ideas all the time, and you, the visiting observer, necessarily become one of these fresh experiences. There are countless examples of the pleasure that individual preschool children, especially boys, take in having a male visitor to their setting. The reason is probably that in the world of some under-fives rewarding contacts with men are all too brief and limited. Early years settings rarely include men and single-parent households are largely led by women.

Should you happen to be a student observer with a visible disability, the children may well be curious and ask questions which, coming from older people, would sound impertinent. At this stage in children's lives this questioning attitude is essential. They must learn to accept disability and you can help. In one instance a visually impaired student, with a guide dog, was regarded as a welcome and interesting visitor, and the children greatly benefited from his periodic calls to tape-record their conversation and play.

The effect on the individuals involved: the adults in the group

Early years settings have a host of different adults associated with them. In a parent-and-toddler group all the parents will be present throughout alongside the leaders, while the health visitor or social worker also may call in from time to time. Preschools, community groups and nursery classes may employ volunteer helpers in addition to paid staff. You may also encounter other students on placement or making child studies. For this reason your personal impact on other adults in these busy places may well be marginal, since you hardly seem to disturb the normal routine. But settings vary, and for some staff seeing the student observer, notebook in hand, may cause anxiety and even arouse suspicion. People working in preschool settings, like anyone else, want others to think well of them. Faced with a student observer they may sense they are being assessed and adapt their behaviour in consequence. Recently one student reported that the staff in the nursery where she was observing reorganised the whole morning's activities to accommodate her, maybe because the student had failed to make clear she wanted to observe the child in a normal morning's programme. On the other hand, many of the adults leading preschools or centres will have once carried out child observations themselves, as part of their training, and hence will be totally understanding and supportive.

The effect on the individuals involved: the parents

In imagining the effect of child observations the lifestyle and cultural traditions of the family cannot be ignored. The stereotypical family, even within any one social class, simply does not exist. So the observer should guard against making assumptions about what the parents might think. Instead listen carefully to what they actually say and watch out for non-verbal clues. You should also take other variables into account. Your observational programme may range from little or no personal involvement with the parents (other than their letter of consent) to the regular weekly visits, over a two-year period, of an intensive Tavistock course. Perhaps the more common experience, however, will be a single observational visit to the child's home to help build up a more rounded picture of the child than could be gained solely by preschool observation.

Parents frequently take pleasure in these student observation visits. In the home setting students rarely come across as authority figures (unlike a health visitor, say). As already hinted, parents may positively welcome the opportunity to talk in detail about their child. They may take pride in the very fact that their child was specially chosen for this study. In practical terms, though, students should recognise that parents often have very little time to spare in a hectic life. Some parents may ask you how their child is faring in the preschool setting. If they do, it is wise to confine your replies to simple statements of fact and otherwise refer them to the preschool team. Try to concentrate on your own task of gathering information. Parents know their own child better than anyone else, and you may pick up intriguing differences between *their* perceptions and those of the preschool staff. Very occasionally parents decline a home visit and this must naturally be accepted. There could be a host of reasons for a refusal.

Whenever home observations are spread over a long period (as in the Tavistock approach), they will doubtless have a greater impact. Parents may have to reorganise their daily schedule around the visits. They will almost inevitably find that the presence of an outsider in the close intimate environment of the family home conditions their general behaviour and responses. Indeed, home observations will tend to make parents more conscious of how they interact with their child and behave 'as parents'.

The effect on the individuals involved: the observer

In seminars students seem to enjoy sharing experiences about their child observations. These experiences are usually positive. The good humour in most preschool settings is infectious and students sometimes re-tell certain episodes with amusement. During observations memories of the student's own childhood may be revived, often happy ones. On occasion, however, less comfortable, even disturbing reminders of the past may re-surface. 'It was', one student remarked, 'the smell of *plasticene* which brought back the horrors of my school-days.' As an observer you may also come to realise the extent to which you are identifying with the child you are watching. In one instance a student was shocked at her partisanship in siding with 'her' child (i.e. the subject of her study) in a squabble over a tricycle. She found herself willing 'her' child to get the tricycle to the extent that, as she put it: 'I didn't care about the other kid'. Students who happen to be parents themselves may draw comparisons with their own offspring or, if their children are older, be reminded of their earlier years.

Your feelings about the observation you have carried out will inevitably be coloured by many factors. Some of these will be personal – your current situation in life, your past experiences, your education and culture. Others will stem from your theoretical standpoint and professional orientation (e.g. towards social work, education or health care), and others again from the circumstances of the observation itself, including your choice of child. Your attitude may even be affected by your willingness to accept observation as a technique, especially in regard to children. Some people do have ethical reservations about watching others in this deliberate way. You should remember, though, that the ultimate purpose of observation is to develop professional competence in work with children and families, and that planning for children's lives must be based on a proper foundation of understanding. From your own point of view, observation should help you to a better understanding of children's efforts at interpreting their world and the range of strategies they use. It may spur you to reassess your own preconceptions and will doubtless sharpen your skills in watching intently and recording accurately. Through these exercises in targeted observation you will, it is hoped, gain in self-confidence as well. (Chapter Eight looks in further detail at the impact on the observer.)

CHAPTER FIVE

Child Observations: Themes and Lines of Enquiry

Introduction

Having collected data from a series of observational visits, what happens next? This chapter introduces the reader to various ways of thinking about the gathered material and is organised around sample themes. Depending on your role in your work situation you will have particular reasons for observation. Social care workers have their special responsibilities for assessment, intervention strategies and investigation of outcomes. Sometimes members of the team around the child will be working collaboratively on the *Common Assessment Framework* (CAF) and sharing their judgements based on observations. Educators use observations to assess and explore young children's sense of well-being, and level of understanding, to study the impact of their own planning and teaching, to follow up concerns about individual children, and to complete the EYFS profile. Health workers too will employ observation in their professional context and to support their quantitative measurements. Students are likely to have broader goals where observation is part of more general study and the development of the necessary observational skills.

Observational methods are valuable when probing particular issues; you may for instance have been studying the different means by which children attract the attention of adults and used the Time Sampling technique. On other occasions, you may have been recording a small section of the daily life of a child, where the child's total behaviour is the subject. In this case you probably followed Naturalistic Observation or the Target Child methods. Whichever techniques have been used you are now ready to examine, reflect on and to analyse the records.

Those particularly interested in the Reggio approach should consult Chapters Nine and Ten on documentation and the hundred languages.

Key issues in development

It is important to grasp certain fundamental characteristics of a child's development. The first concerns the dramatic speed of growth, physical, social and mental, that occurs in the early years of life. Picture in your mind's eye a new-born baby, a small 16-inch-long, wrapped-up 'bundle', about eight pounds in weight. While certainly 'programmed' for rapid development, the infant just now seems immature and fragile. Now picture a five-year-old in the school playground, organising other children in a complicated imaginative game. Chattering and gesticulating, she races across the play area and climbs nimbly up a climbing frame – already displaying considerable mobility and physical co-ordination, advanced skills in language, competence in the 'rules' of social relationships, and growing in all-round competence. Progress will never be so rapid again. The significance of the early years has been recognised and reinforced through the EPPE research (Sylva *et al.* 2004) and has already been enshrined in government legislation. Billions of pounds are being spent in advancing early education.

The second crucial feature of development is the drive (intrinsic motivation) to explore, to find out and to master the environment. The power of this force should not be underestimated. We see it all the time in children's curiosity and in their play. Jerome Bruner, in a classic chapter, 'Nature and Uses of Immaturity' (1975), highlights the value of a long period of playful immaturity, as a necessary foundation of mature behaviour in adulthood. Indeed, of all the animal kingdom, humans have the longest period of immaturity and vulnerability. Human beings are also remarkable for their adaptability and flexibility, features that have enabled them to exploit endless opportunities and to 'colonise' just about every environment on the planet. In part this adaptability is due to their direct experiential learning ability, but they can also learn by imitation and by proxy – in other words through others' experiences. They can also be taught.

The third aspect of development worth highlighting is just how unique and individual every child is. The variety is astonishing and results from the differing combinations of genes and experiences, the constant interaction of the biological and the environmental. Parents regularly comment on the differences among their own offspring, perhaps not recognising that, for each member of the family, life experiences within that family may be altogether different, even though the genetic inheritance is similar. Thus, the first-born is the sole focus of inexperienced parental attention, whereas the second-born enters an established family with parents who are no longer novices at the job. Because each child is unique, observers should always avoid generalising about behaviour on the basis of a single child. Differences between children also relate to the cultural framework in which they grow up. The EYFS takes the 'unique child' as one of its four principles. But in emphasising uniqueness it should not be forgotten that a child is a social being. The EYFS emphasis perhaps fails to notice that children are naturally programmed to participate in social groups. This aspect should not be ignored and is one of the themes of this chapter. Another central issue – the holistic nature of development, a matter that is certainly recognised by both the *Every Child Matters* agenda and the EYFS.

Figure 5.1, while highlighting the chief features of development, is of course a drastic simplification of a dynamic process. Human beings are complex. There are many sides to our personalities, abilities and interests; most of us would strongly object to being thought of as one dimensional.

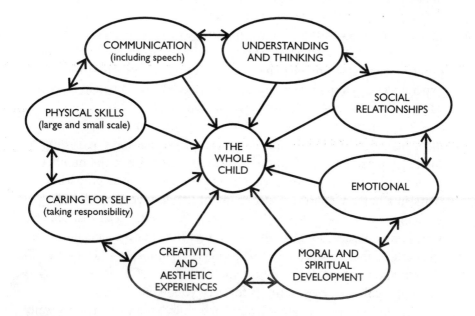

Figure 5.1. A holistic view of the developing child

In addition, the different categories isolated in the diagram all interact in ways far more complicated than represented by the links shown. A 'holistic' view recognises this complexity. (Chapter Ten on the 'hundred languages' also reinforces the idea of interlinked ways of thinking and communicating ideas, feelings and experiences.)

Reflection on themes

From a Naturalistic Observation or using the *Target Child* method, you will have collected material to examine from many angles. As a student you may be asked to choose a particular theme that interests you and then to use your observations, to read the relevant literature, and finally to reflect on the issues from different points of view. The themes identified below are merely a sample illustrating possible lines of study.

1. Attachment and well-being

Human infants depend utterly on adult help. Babies and young children require food, shelter, protection, love and care of every kind. For sheer survival they simply must have ways of engaging and retaining adult attention. They need to be in close proximity to the adults they so much depend on. The adults must be able to tune in, pick up signals and respond to individual needs. The 'attachment' that develops between parents (or whoever stands in for the parents) and their infants has been briefly described in Chapter Three, and indeed from an evolutionary point of view attachment behaviour makes real sense. How the infant experiences this nurturing attention is very vividly explained in *Why Love Matters: How affection shapes a baby's brain* (Gerhardt 2004).

You will almost certainly notice young children displaying attachment behaviour – i.e. keeping in contact in various ways according to their age, personality and culture. Given the large rise in the number of babies and toddlers in group care, many students will be preparing for work in a nursery context. Since many of the very young children they encounter will not yet be fluent speakers, adults need particularly well-honed observational skills to interpret the children's meaning, not to speak of the empathy required to make relationships. Peter Elfer, in 'Observation observed' (in Abbott and Langston 2005), looks closely at these particular issues in settings for very young children.

The 'key person' system – where each child has a worker specifically allocated – has now been fully accepted and is a component part of the

EYFS. Without a sense of being connected to specific adults small children are at risk of not developing well either mentally or physically. Elfer and Dearnley (2007) recognise that this close relationship is very demanding for staff and therefore advocate better professional training that explores psychoanalytic issues.

Through the reactions of others, with in or outside the family, very young children learn to recognise their own strong emotions. Paul Harris has reviewed the processes by which this happens. In his article 'The child's understanding of emotion' (1994) he summarises research on children who have experienced two types of distorted or extreme emotional environments – one in which the person primarily responsible for the child's care was suffering from chronic depression, the other characterised by angry family rows as the family split up. Depressed adults can blight children's confidence and self-esteem simply through their low threshold of irritability, their unenthusiastic reactions and their failure to respond and show interest. This may set up poor behaviour patterns so that when the children face novel situations in the future they may be resistant or unwilling to respond. Aggressive environments may often have especially negative consequences. To protect themselves the children sometimes become very still, passive and intensely watchful, seemingly almost frozen, or else might smile excessively as if continuing to placate the violent actors in scenes of domestic violence (even if they themselves were not the target).

It is interesting how children reveal their emotions through body language as well as verbal cues. How they interpret other people's feelings may well relate to their own family's expression of emotions, which can vary enormously. Some children will acquire an extensive vocabulary and ability to describe feelings and meanings, while others will not.

2. Settling in

What does the experience of joining a group (crèche, nursery, preschool or whatever) mean to the very young child? Much will depend on the child's age and previous experiences. But the possible shock of the event should not be underestimated, and observations of a young child at this crucial time may be disturbing to the observer. The Tavistock model may be the best tool for this task because it should pick up the miniscule non-verbal signs of the inner feelings of the child: how he holds himself,

UNIVERSITY OF WINCHESTER
LIBRARY

where he glances, his facial expressions, how he uses his body in relation to others, i.e. coming forward or holding back.

Other variables will also affect settling in, such as the child's age, whether a sibling has been a member, and whether the newcomer already has friends in the setting. The group policy on settling children in is also highly significant in making the transition from home an easy one. It is common to arrange a series of accompanied preliminary visits by the child and parent before the proper starting date. These allow the child to become accustomed to the place, the people and the activities on offer. Parents may also stay for a few sessions, or part of sessions, to help their child adjust comfortably. Yet even with all these helpful opportunities the experience of settling in can be stressful.

Take the example of a three-year-old entering the busy world of 24 other children. It could be a major event. Some children may have come from quiet, fairly solitary backgrounds. Until now they have perhaps met relatively few other children, and even those who did have more play-mates may have played with them in quite small groups. Settling in may also be harder for children who have recently suffered major changes in their lives. A child who has been hospitalised for instance, or undergone a family break-up, a house move, or even the birth of a fresh sibling, might find adjustment extra hard.

It should not be too difficult to empathise with the new child by recalling our own feelings as an adult coming into a group of strangers. We are likely to have behaved much as the child will. Five reactions are characteristic. The first is watchfulness. The newcomer is likely to spend a great deal of time simply looking around at what is going on, observing the other children, seizing on clues about what to do, where to go, what is allowed, and so on. Besides the many people that have to be made sense of, there are also all the activities. The leaders will have tried to make the play seem enticing, but the newcomer may still be unsure what it involves. Just watching the children most familiar with the materials may seem the safest bet. Stillness, the second type of reaction you may observe, is asso-ciated with the watching, for you can only keep watch if you remain rea-sonably stationary. Children may sit just out of the action for as much as an hour, simply 'taking it all in'. In contrast, some newcomers exhibit a third behaviour pattern. They run to the other extreme and flit like a but-terfly around the room, perhaps handling a few objects as they go, but avoiding involvement in anything. Drawing a simple plan of the layout of the play room would allow you to plot the child's movements in such a case. Studying this later can reveal the extent of flitting behaviour.

A fourth type of behaviour common among new arrivals at this age is the unwillingness to engage in conversation. Once again empathy will help, since adults in unfamiliar situations likewise tend to 'play safe' and do more listening than talking. Finally, children often reveal their uncertainties about a strange preschool situation by anxiety signs. Familiar examples of such traits include fiddling with hair or clothes, thumb-sucking, cuddling a soft toy or clinging to a reminder from home (a bit of blanket perhaps).

In his classic book, *An Ethological Study of Children's Behaviour* (1972), McGrew identified four of these modes of behaviour – just watching, lack of activity, little talk and use of a comforter. To these four modes it is certainly worth adding 'butterfly-like' flitting. Your observation may pick up yet other signals.

As a topic for a case study, the adaptation of a child into a new environment, covered by means of a series of observations over a few months, has much to recommend it. You are likely to observe changes in the kinds of behaviour described above. You may also notice how friendships with individual children develop and which activities seem most effective in easing the child into this new life. Most importantly you will perceive how particular forms of adult support help to establish the child as a participating member of the group.

Comparing the child's use of language over a period (say from the first week of arrival to two months later) can be equally instructive. You may discover how much your child talks to adults as opposed to children, and whether he or she talks mainly to one person. You might examine what sorts of conversations are engaged in and how language is used. The adjustments that some children have to make, especially children newly arrived in this country (possibly as refugees), are potentially enormous. While preschool settings are supposed to be sensitive to the cultural origins of every child, there are still uncertainties in implementing this requirement. Helpful guidance will be found in Hazareesingh *et al.* (1989) and Siraj-Blatchford (1994).

3. Social development and cultural context

Preschool experiences may be extremely valuable in social development. A large and growing body of research illuminates this aspect of

development and is reinforcing our understanding of the crucial importance of social relationships in personality growth. In Chapter Three you
may have read about Vygotsky's theories, which have continued to be
developed. Barbara Rogoff's latest book (2003) is the most important in
this field.

Your personal observations should give you insights into social relationships. The Target Child method (Sylva *et al.* 1980, p.137) in particular can be a handy tool for concentrating on interactions in a group
setting. It is straightforward to use. Under the column labelled *SOCIAL*
you enter the social code for each minute of observation. By coding in
this way you create a summary of the child's social interaction or lack of
it. The *social code* (derived from Sylva 1980, pp.237–239) is simple to
grasp:

SOL   solitary

PAIR   two people together (child plus another child)

SG   in a small group of three to five children

LG   in a large group of six or more children

/P   'parallel' – the child is plays alone but close to another
        child or group.

For instance PAIR/P means that the child plays near another child but
quite independently. The children may all be doing the same thing, but
the code /P should be used unless they are interacting. A circle drawn
round PAIR, SG or LG indicates that an adult is involved. Thus PAIR
means that the child is playing or chatting with an adult. Having added
the social codes to your observation, you can tally the amount of time
spent in the various groupings. This information could be made into a bar
graph, a Venn diagram or some other format that displays the proportions
of time.

A very influential study by Parten (1933) – though one based on a
single nursery – suggests that children move through stages in their play as
they grow older. Indeed it was this study that coined the phrase 'parallel
play'. Parten's categories of play begin with the unoccupied child,
followed by the child as onlooker, and then (in order) the child involved
in solitary or independent play, taking part in parallel activity, in associa-
tive play, and finally in co-operative play. There is a tendency for children
to move through these various stages but naturally they are an over-sim-

plification. What may be more significant than the child's age is her or his newness in any particular group. It is also important to note the *quality* of the involvement with other people and the effect adults may have on a child's activity. The active interest shown by an adult often increases the length of time a child sticks with a task. Adults may legitimately 'scaffold' (Vygotsky and Bruner) the child's activity by providing suitable materials, perhaps by subdividing the task and by offering positive suggestions, but definitely not by taking over.

The second and third years of life produce dramatic changes in a child's capacity to understand social rules. Of course the rules and social conventions in a preschool group may well contrast, or even conflict, with those at home. Observers will notice that, in general, children seem to adapt to routines remarkably quickly, but there may be times when they face a confusing dilemma. Father says 'stand up and fight for yourself', in stark contradiction to the 'no-fighting' rule of the group. An Asian child might be told by preschool staff not to make tea in a saucepan, when that is what she observes her mother doing every day.

The role of their peer group for children's experience does not always receive sufficient attention. In the Reggio preschools, however, learning is seen as essentially a group process and children are supported in their collaborative projects. In the context of the family, children learn much more from their brothers and sisters than might be imagined given the emphasis usually placed on the parental contribution. Judy Dunn's observations of siblings in their families have produced some very revealing insights (Dunn 1988, 1993).

Social interactions among preschool children go beyond just adapting to a group, learning how to share and making friends. Children's cognitive development actually depends on social experiences. Learning not only about the social but also the physical world comes about largely through our interactions with other people, especially the members of our own cultural group. The work of Vygotsky (see Chapter Three) has strengthened our understanding of the process by which this probably happens. He believed that from the very moment of birth the child should share in group experiences. Children learn language, how to solve problems and about the environment through these interactions. Vygotsky's famous phrase 'what a child can do with assistance to-day, she will be able to do by herself to-morrow' epitomises the nature of the learning process. The child is in the position of an apprentice. The more competent members of the group (adults and older children) 'scaffold' the child's learning experiences. Vygotsky insisted that all learning is located in a cultural milieu. (For further reading about this see Rogoff (2003)

Finally, a thought from Hazareesingh *et al.* (1989) on distinctive cultural viewpoints. Twenty-first-century British society is very individualistic. We encourage children to be competitive rather than co-operative and we see childhood as separate from the adult world. Other cultures may regard children differently. Consider Hazareesingh's statement from the perspective of Indian philosophy: 'the child should not be simply "brought up": there is an accompanying responsibility for the adult to enter into the child's mode of experiencing the world' (p.18).

4. Communication

Fluent communication through language by the age of five years is miraculous, and yet virtually everyone achieves this in whatever culture they grow up. So fascinating and puzzling is this skill that more has been written about language than about any other area of development. We use language for just about everything – to obtain what we need, to explain ourselves, to make friends, to solve problems, to entertain ourselves, to study and learn. If you have been observing children from one to four years old the talk you have been hearing comes from children in their most dramatic phase of language development. What should you have been looking out for? A few suggestions are offered here. Some are more concerned with the stages of development, others with the circumstances that may encourage the acquisition of this essential skill.

You may first notice actual *speech production*: the clarity of the sounds, perhaps certain mispronunciations or even omissions of parts of words, which may strike you as interesting. Whether this is just a normal stage in speech growth, a problem relating to the enunciation of speech sounds, or an indication of some other difficulty (such as hearing loss) is not always easy to establish. Next to the mechanics of sound production, a subject of considerable fascination, is the child's use of *grammar*, or *syntax* as linguists call it. Steven Pinker's *The Language Instinct* (1994) gives an account of how humans learn to use language. Drawing on the work of Noam Chomsky, Pinker claims that language is innate – that every human being is born not only with a special capacity to acquire language, but with a facility for grammar. Just how far humans are pre-programmed in this manner remains controversial, but the ready way that children take to spoken language cannot be doubted. Language can be compared with walking, in that almost all children will learn it without actually being taught how, though they need to be in an environment where people are regularly speaking.

In your observations you may want to consider the kinds of grammatical structures the children are using. Are they at the single-word stage? Are they employing telegraphic speech (where just key words are used, such as: Where Mummy gone?)? You may well find examples of over-extended or over-generalised rules, as in 'She goed to her Mum,' where the child applies the normal rule for forming the past tense to what happens to be an irregular verb. What is remarkable at this stage is how much children get right. Pinker points out that in order to apply the suffix (the word endings) properly in English you have to understand four sorts of distinction:

1. *I* walk but *he* walks ('first person' versus 'third person')

2. He *walks* but they *walk* (singular versus plural)

3. He *walks* but he *walked* (present tense versus past tense)

4. He *walks* to school, but he is *walking* to school (simple present versus continuous present).

It seems confusing, yet more than 90 per cent of three-and-a-half year-olds manage to use the correct form (Pinker 1994, p.44).

Another topic you might consider is *language style and purposes*. How exactly are children using language at this phase of their development? Do they talk only about the here and now or the future and past as well? How do they join in conversations? Closely associated with the styles of language are the *situations which encourage conversation*. Do children talk much to other children? Do they talk more when they are in large or small groups? What kinds of activities give rise to conversation? Gordon Wells' (1987) research, based on recordings made in children's own homes, found that the circumstances that correlated with 'good' language development depended on attentive, sensitive adults supporting their children's own efforts. Beyond that, the family practice of telling and reading stories at the preschool stage was associated with children being able to read by the age of seven.

If you are able to observe in both the home and group settings you will be able to compare the communication patterns in these two environments. Tizard and Hughes (1984) researched this aspect, though observing girls only. They found striking differences and, to the dismay of some nursery teachers, discerned that the language used by children in the nursery school was far less complex. Cultural differences between home and the group setting, including language use, can be huge. With bilingual or multilingual children this contrast will be accentuated, because they will be variously competent in two or more languages according to their family and social background. In some Pakistani families Panjabi would be the mother tongue, Urdu the formal language and Arabic the language used in religion, all on top of the English they use for communication outside the home (Siraj-Blatchford 1994). In the preschool settings you might compare the child's use of language while occupied in different activities – for instance playing with unstructured materials (like drawing and clay) as compared with playing with standardised toys such as jigsaw puzzles. Does the bilingual child use her/his own home language at all in the preschool setting? A related question asks what encouragement is given to communication in the child's mother tongue by way of bilingual books and preschool staff who are themselves bilingual.

5. Sustained shared thinking

The *Effective Provision of Pre-school Provision* (EPPE, Sylva *et al.* 2004) and *Researching Effective Pedagogy in the Early Years* (REPEY, Siraj-Blatchford *et al.* 2002) research projects have been major factors in shaping the government's policy for children's services and are of European significance. EPPE explored those characteristics of preschool provision that affect young children's development, particularly addressing intellectual and social aspects. The sample was large, with over 3000 children between the ages of three and seven years, and information was gathered both on the children and from their parents, in home environments and in the preschool settings. These settings covered a wide range, including day nurseries and schools in all kinds of localities. REPEY made a close study of effective practice in a limited number of settings chosen because their children appeared to be making good to excellent developmental progress in the preschool years. The findings from these two projects are enlightening as regards understanding the conditions that lead to 'good outcomes' for children. In the context of this book the most important conclusions were that:

- cognitive and social development are complementary; one should not be prioritised over the other
- children should enjoy a mixture of adult-led and freely chosen play
- adult–child interactions that involve 'sustained shared thinking' and open-ended questioning extend children's capacity
- staff must support children in rationalising and talking through any conflicts they have
- settings should provide differentiated learning opportunities to meet the needs of individual children – taking into consideration cultural, bilingual and gender differences and 'special educational needs'.

The idea of 'sustained shared thinking' has evoked a strong response. The EPPE research demonstrated that young children learn most effectively when an adult and child, or alternatively two children, work together in an intellectual way to solve a problem, clarify a concept or extend a narrative. You might try to pinpoint examples of sustained shared thinking in your observations.

6. Concentration and involvement

Concentration is obviously an essential requirement in learning, one of several traits that we sometimes call 'learning dispositions'. Margaret Carr, a government adviser in New Zealand, has been influential in alerting educators to young children's learning dispositions (Carr 2001), especially these five:

- taking an interest
- willingness to become involved
- persisting with difficulty or uncertainty
- communication with others
- taking responsibility.

She has also worked with Guy Claxton in the UK on this question of learning dispositions (Carr and Claxton 2004). It is to Ferre Laevers in Belgium, however, that we look for detailed descriptions of the dispositions that are most likely to promote learning (Laevers 1994; Pascal and Bertram 1997). His research at the Centre for Experimental

Education at Leuven University has demonstrated that the highest outcomes are achieved when the educational setting truly values the child's seemingly playful enquiries and deep engagement in whatever he or she is doing, thus enhancing the child's feelings of efficacy and confidence. Laevers' approach matches Vygotsky's concept of 'scaffolding', i.e. that adults should support rather than direct children's cognitive growth. Children have enormous energy when motivated by their own exploratory drive, as is clear from their boundless natural curiosity. Laevers therefore is critical of the emphasis given to prescribed curricula in schools, neglecting this disposition to explore. In his view it is the exploratory drive that guarantees life-long learning since it seems to generate intense forms of concentration. When people are thoroughly engaged they reach 'a state of joy, creativity and total involvement' that is sometimes described as 'flow'. People lose track of time: 'problems seem to disappear and there is an exhilarating feeling of transcendence' (Csikszentmihalyi 2002, back cover). This applies to adults as much as to children but children's play especially often attains this state of 'flow' so releasing energy and powering brain development. But this cannot happen unless children feel at ease, self-confident and able to act spontaneously (Laevers' definition of 'well-being'). In Laevers' opinion their 'physical needs, the need for tenderness and affection, the need for safety and clarity, the need for social recognition, the need to feel competent and the need for meaning and moral value in life' must all be satisfied (Laevers 2000, p.24).

At the same time children must be thoroughly caught up in their play activity, and here Laevers has identified nine 'signals of involvement':

- concentration: the main indicator being eye movements

- energy: not to be confused with the release of pent-up energy, this is mental energy

- complexity and creativity: more than routine behaviour – the child adds an individual touch

- facial expression and posture: look for non-verbal signs, including overall posture

- persistence: children who are really involved do not easily let go of the action, and are not readily distracted

- precision: involved children give special attention to their work; those non-involved tend to race through

- reaction time: children are alert and express their motivation
- verbal utterances: they offer spontaneous comments, enthusiastic descriptions, they seem to be unable to refrain from putting into words what they are experiencing
- satisfaction: their pleasure in the experience is evident.

While it is generally best to limit the use checklists and scales in studies of this sort they sometimes have a place. The following scale derived from Laevers' work is worth considering, especially since it may help you enlarge your vocabulary for describing your observations. Called the 'Leuven Involvement Scale for Young Children' (LIS-YC), it is designed to assess children's 'involvement' in early years settings.

LEVEL 1 – NO ACTIVITY

The child is not engaged or participant, shows little energy, seems absent-minded, may stare into space (but beware, this could equally be a sign of inner concentration); the child may repeat stereotyped, simple actions.

LEVEL 2 – FREQUENTLY INTERRUPTED ACTIVITY

The child is engaged in some activity but for half of the observed period displays non-activity, and may even wander off, with concentration interrupted.

LEVEL 3 – MAINLY CONTINUOUS ACTIVITY

The child is busy at a routine level, seems partially involved, but displays little intensity and is easily distracted.

LEVEL 4 – CONTINUOUS ACTIVITY WITH SOME INTENSE MOMENTS

The activity has real meaning for the child who concentrates hard for most of the time. There may be short moments of distraction but the child soon returns to the activity.

LEVEL 5 – SUSTAINED INTENSE ACTIVITY

The child shows continuous and intense activity. The essential components of concentration, creativity, energy and persistence are all obvious. This last level is an example of 'flow' as described above.

7. Schemas

An understanding of schemas has proved valuable for all workers with young children besides being illuminating for parents. Schemas may be defined as repeated behaviour patterns spontaneously adopted by the child. These are normal and necessary, not obsessive, actions. In fact repetitive behaviour encourages the development of neural structures in the brain. The idea came originally from the biologist and epistemologist Jean Piaget, who noted that not only did young children learn about the world through their physical activity but that these very actions had an effect on their growing brains. In particular brain structures and understanding of spatial organisation are formed through schematic behaviour (see below). Chris Athey's (1990) research on schemas incorporating parents' own observations led the way towards a wider use of the concept.

Observed schemas in children's play include repeated movements, drawing the same things over and over, and reiterating the same phrases in speech, but there are many others (see Nutbrown 2006a). Common ones will be recognised in children's behaviour such as:

- turning round and round, or moving objects in a circular motion, or drawing circular shapes – 'rotation' schema

- covering things up, or hiding, or scribbling over a drawing – 'enveloping' schema

- linking things together – 'connecting' schema

- throwing objects, or jumping up and down, or drawing vertical lines – 'trajectory' schema

- taking toys from one place to another or playing with vehicles – 'transporting' schema.

Some 20 such schemas have been distinguished. An example from Nutbrown (2006a) helps to show the nature of an 'enclosing' schema.

> Belinda was three years old and she seemed to be tuned into spotting or seeking out opportunities to enclose or be enclosed, and objects which enclose. At home she enjoyed emptying and filling the washing machine, and in the garden and in the bath she filled numerous containers with water to the point that they overflowed. She and her mother built up a collection of tins and boxes that she enjoyed fitting inside one another in different combinations and she often enjoyed sitting inside

cardboard boxes used to carry home the shopping from the supermarket, sometimes pretending that the box was a car, bus, boat or rocket. ...' The adults around Belinda supported her interests which led into stories and mathematical skills concerned with space and ordering. (Nutbrown 2006a, p.128)

In another case (Nutbrown 2006a) a 17–month-old boy seemed to be obsessed with pushing buttons and similar actions. Worryingly he tried to switch on appliances such as the television and cooker but his mother, having learned about schemas, gave him toys that allowed him to keep on pressing buttons in safety.

The importance of schemas for brain development has been underestimated. Research on mathematics and young children reveals convincingly how the repeated exploration of spatial relationships leads to the formation of mathematical concepts (Carruthers and Worthington 2006). Your observations will very probably turn up other examples of repeated schema behaviour. If you wish to pursue this topic the best recent book is *Threads of Thinking: Young children's learning and the role of early education* (Nutbrown 2006b).

8. Perspectives on gender

Interest in the differing characteristics of females and males is pretty well universal. Observations of children regularly provoke discussions based on comparisons of girls and boys in their choice of toys, their types of play and their general behaviour. The debate usually brings up the perennial question of the relative contribution of biological inheritance and social environment. Without doubt social conditioning begins from the moment of birth. Parents of new-borns are sometimes inclined to refer to boy babies as 'big' and 'strong' whereas girls are talked of as being 'pretty'. Blue for a boy and pink for a girl reflects the same attitude. But more recent scientific research, reported in Michael Gurian's book *Boys and Girls Learn Differently: A guide for teachers and parents* (2001), now indicates that hormonal influences, even in the womb, produce differences in the mental development of girls and boys. In the early years 'girls talk sooner, develop better vocabularies, read better and have better fine motor skills. Boys, on the other hand, have better auditory memory, are better at three-dimensional reasoning, are more prone to explore, and achieve greater abstract design after puberty' (from Gurian's book cover blurb). Teachers and parents would do well to recognise these variations.

The subtle and diverse influences that guide a child's discovery of gender difference and consequent differences in behaviour are everywhere – through role models within the immediate family and community, through social contacts among children of the same age group, through she/he distinctions in everyday speech, through the packaging of toys and foodstuffs, and through the media. We know that children become aware of the concept of gender from a very early age. Between 12 and 24 months children have already teased out the gender difference between their mother and father and between boys and girls. They use the correct labels – girl, boy, woman, man, she, he – from two years onwards. From three to five years they achieve greater stability of the concept, aware that they themselves will retain the same gender throughout their lives. Finally they come to understand the notion of constancy, that while outward appearances may change, the gender of a person remains constant.

The sophistication of children's awareness of their social environment, and of gender roles in particular, before they start school has come to be recognised only quite recently. Children observe and absorb the adult world, but it would be wrong to assume that it is purely a matter of adults conditioning children. Barrie Thorne (1993) found through extensive research that, far from learning about the world solely from adults, children increasingly 'teach' each other (p.3).

Choice of playthings may seem a simple indicator of gender stereotypes. Certainly you may see more boys than girls playing with large wooden bricks, and *vice versa* with dolls, but in their review of research Henshall and McGuire (1986) make three points which should help observers guard against over-generalising. First, the nature and ethos of the preschool setting affect the pattern of toy use. Next, they claim that 'children actually spend most of their time playing with toys which are not gender-differentiated' (p.39). Finally they conclude that *gender differences* are not necessarily *gender preferences*. If boys did play with building blocks more than girls, girls nonetheless played with building blocks three times as much as they did with dolls. The relative use of toys by the two gender groups is worth thinking about, as is the use of play areas. Boys are often expected to 'let off steam' and may be allowed to play on more adventurous apparatus. They may also receive less comforting than girls when they hurt themselves, though boys do tend to attract more attention than girls overall. On the other hand, girls are viewed as showing more empathy than boys, in being responsive to other people's needs and acting helpfully. The children themselves probably recognise the same distinction.

A final gender feature worth looking out for is the choice of same-sex play partners. From around the age of three or four children show a preference for play with members of their own sex. Nonetheless, preschool staff should find ways to encourage play in mixed groups so that boys and girls learn to value each others' experiences.

It should also be borne in mind that early years settings are almost entirely staffed by women. What might the consequences of this be in conditioning gender behaviour and the development of self-identity?

A final note

This chapter has covered only a few sample themes. Many others could be explored, among them the nature of children's imaginative play, especially between the ages of three and six years. Children seem to be natural storytellers; they switch between fact and fantasy all the time. A leading authority on this subject is Vivian Gussin Paley, see particularly her book *A Child's Work: The importance of fantasy play* (2004). Here she recalls stories children have told her and enters deeply into their meanings. This book memorably concludes with children's stories that play out their anxieties after seeing TV images of the 9/11 Twin Towers disaster.

CHAPTER SIX

Preschool Contexts
for Observation in England

Introduction

This chapter presents a snapshot of English preschool services in late 2008. Children are required by law to recieve education in the term following their fifth birthday, though this might be education at home. Parents are required by law to ensure that their child receives full time education suitable for the child's age, ability and aptitude. It is interesting to note that most other countries have chosen the sixth birthday as the starting age for statutory schooling. In practice a large proportion of British children start during the year in which they become five, entering the reception class when they are still four years old.

A long-awaited and truly radical transformation commenced in the UK in 2003, but each constituent part – England, Scotland, Wales and Northern Ireland – has somewhat different systems. For many years there existed a fragmentary patchwork of preschool services (usually part-time), lacking coherent strategy, divided between care and education services, and with publicly funded care only for children 'in need'. Central government viewed the upbringing of children before school age as essentially a private family matter (see Jackson and Fawcett 2009), but this picture has almost completely changed in the last few years.

Though the Labour government came into power in 1997 it was not until six years later that legislative reform began. Several different pressures for change brought about a fresh, more comprehensive approach – many years of lobbying by early years advocates; unfavourable comparisons with European early years practice; awareness of the inequities of the UK system where good-quality provision was not necessarily available to families who needed it most; the gap between children who succeed and those who do not; and the government's increasing concerns about family poverty. In the end it seems that two significant events compelled the Treasury to act. One was the publication of Lord Laming's report (2003) identifying the serious lack of co-ordination of services for young children, the other powerful research evidence showing the effectiveness of early education (Sylva *et al.* 2004). The first of these, the Laming report, concerned the horrific death of Victoria Climbié (already mentioned in Chapter One). The second document – *Effective Provision of Pre-school Education* (EPPE) – demonstrated that 'quality preschool education can ameliorate the effects of disadvantage by increasing children's learning attainment thereby reducing the effects of social exclusion' (Siraj-Blatchford 2009, and also described in Chapter Five of this book).

Government action began with the *Every Child Matters* (ECM) agenda in 2003 when the five 'outcomes for children' were established: being healthy, staying safe, enjoying and achieving, making a positive contribution, and economic well-being. Professionals generally maintain, of course, that they have always held such priorities for children. Nevertheless the ECM agenda is helping to establish a culture that focuses on children's well-being, and further relevant legislation is being put in place to this effect. *Choice for Parents, the Best Start for Children: A ten year strategy* (HMT 2004) took a broad view, addressing six areas:

- the first year of life
- the positive effects of early education
- the relationship of quality services to children's outcomes – social, emotional and cognitive
- the needs of disadvantaged children as the chief beneficiaries of early education
- the tackling of the causes of poverty
- the quality of the home learning environment.

This strategy led to local authority reorganisation into what are now called Children's Trusts or Local Area Partnerships, charged with improving the outcomes for all children but in particular narrowing the gap between those who achieve and those who do not. Education, health and social care services have been reconfigured and integrated. Schools hours are currently being extended with 'wrap-around' care facilities to allow women to work in the belief that this will help reduce family poverty.

More recently the aspirational *Children's Plan* (DCSF 2007b) set the target of England becoming 'the best place in the world for children and young people to grow up'. The strategic objectives are:

- to secure the health and well-being of children and young people
- to safeguard the young and vulnerable
- to close the gap in educational achievement for children from disadvantaged backgrounds
- to ensure that young people are participating and achieving their potential up to 18 and beyond
- to keep children and young people on the path to success.

Schools are at the heart of the strategy, but for the 'early years' – the general term to cover the period from birth to five – establishing an integrated Children's Centre in every community is the main long-term goal. It is intended that these centres will cater for all aspects of the child's and family's needs, including day care, early education, health, family support services, ante-natal services and so on. Rolling out the plans has been proceeding for some time by either remodelling existing centres or establishing new ones. In practice, disadvantaged communities were the first to receive 'Sure Start Children's Centres', of which about 2500 had been established in England by the start of 2009. These centres are still (in early 2009) very disparate in the quantity and type of services they provide. Moreover they require staffing by a highly skilled workforce working across professional boundaries. Given government financial constraints, implementing these ambitious and expensive plans will take a long time.

Meanwhile, for families outside nominated disadvantaged communities, the mix of services for young children remains much as it was, comprising services originally provided by local education authorities (nursery schools and nursery classes in primary schools) and the private, voluntary and independent (PVI) sector (preschools, nurseries and independent schools as well as more informal services such as parent and toddler groups). 'In essence the ten-year strategy is designed to rationalise, redesign and re-badge the existing early years initiatives so that they fit within the ECM framework and become a coherent strategy for improving the quality of services' (Owen 2006, p.189). Within these early years settings there are still very significant variations, including the ages and grouping of the children, the physical circumstances (buildings, the availability of outside play space, the range and quality of equipment and play materials) and above all, in the training, the quality and the philosophy of the adults in charge.

As part of the centralisation and standardisation of all early years services the government has, from September 2008, required every type of care and education services, including childminding, to follow the *Early Years Foundation Stage* (EYFS). This is legally binding and enforced by Ofsted (Office for Standards in Education) inspections. This radical departure, setting out curriculum guidance for children from birth to five, is unique to England. No other country has ever attempted such detailed and comprehensive direction. The main contents of the EYFS are set out in Chapter One in this book while the philosophy is discussed in Chapter Two.

Early years services

This section relates solely to England since Wales, Northern Ireland and Scotland all display different characteristics. As a student visitor you should be alert to the expectations of the EYFS curriculum for absolutely everyone working in the children's services. At the same time you should appreciate that these services are still patchy and uneven in quality. While certain services are free, the majority have to be paid for by parents, and in some cases the cost is high. However the nursery education grant entitles three- and four-year-old children to 15 hours of free nursery education per week, and is to be extended to two-year-olds. Any setting is eligible for the grant providing the requirements of government are met; in practice virtually all services are part of the scheme. Full day care (over and beyond the 15 hours) needed by working parents is not free, and nurseries providing the necessary longer hours are usually expensive. Most working parents therefore still turn to childminders for day care.

The actual choice for parents is still likely to depend on where they live, their financial situation, their access to transport, and the actual range of provision locally, rather than their personal preferences about what is best for their child. For many families it may well be that practicalities in the end over-ride any other priorities such as quality of care and education.

Seven types of early years setting are described below, each starting with a note about the ages of children attending and the settings' typical opening times. All are now registered with and inspected by Ofsted so that the same regulations about ratios of adults to children, staffing qualifications, space required and equipment apply equally to all.

1. Preschools, playgroups and community nurseries

Ages of children: 2 to 4 years
Opening times: often 2 or 3 weekly sessions of 2–3 hours during school terms

By far the majority of children in the UK attend preschools, otherwise called playgroups or perhaps community groups or the equivalent. The history of preschool playgroups began in 1961 with a parent's letter to the *Guardian* newspaper arguing the need to provide for more play and social opportunities for children given the lack of nursery schools across the country, and suggesting that parents themselves should take the initiative. The writer was flooded with letters and in response the playgroup movement took off. Preschool playgroups can now be found across the whole UK, though they are more common in rural areas. They seldom have exclusive use of premises and commonly use village and church halls. Sometimes spare classrooms in schools are available to accommodate preschools, while a few have their own purpose-built premises, and others are run in private houses. The adults leading preschools come from many backgrounds but almost always are parents themselves. Some may have received a teaching, nursing or Nursery Nurses Examination Board (NNEB) training, but they are now more likely to have gained either a preschool course diploma from the Preschool Learning Alliance (PLA, formerly the Preschool Playgroups Association) or else a National Vocational Qualification (NVQ). It is essential to recognise that the playgroup course, though well respected, is part-time and of a very different nature from the academic discipline of a four-year degree.

Preschool leaders and their assistants are generally paid, though at a meagre rate, and will be helped by unpaid adult volunteers – probably parents attending on a rota system. These parent helpers, and parental involvement in general, have traditionally been central to the playgroup movement ethos. It was due to the energetic drive of many parents (largely, but not entirely women) during the 1960s and 1970s that playgroups mushroomed. These parents discovered that by 'doing-it-them-selves' they gained in personal confidence, skills and understanding. They learned a lot about children in particular, about the crucial impor-tance of 'play' and how best to promote it. They found out how to run a committee and manage finances, and how to negotiate with local authori-ties. The picture is now changing however, since many women expect to return to paid employment as soon as possible after the birth of their children. In consequence, to recruit even paid staff has become increas-ingly difficult, let alone the voluntary helpers prepared to work regularly.

These groups are part of the voluntary sector and receive very little public money, though the government's scheme for the funding of early years education for a limited number of hours (currently 15 hours a week for three- and four-year-olds) has helped to some degree towards making ends meet. Otherwise parents' fees have to cover the costs of rent, heating, salaries and materials. Many groups are community-run charities and others are private businesses, with the fees naturally reflecting the nature of the organisation.

Playgroups originally modelled themselves on the traditional nursery school and some provide children with a rich, well-equipped environ-ment in the care of enthusiastic, sensitive adults. The quality of the staff overall is very variable though. In addition, the premises may be barely adequate. The children may have to play on dubious village hall floors and even use adult toilets, while playgroup staff must sometimes carry equipment to and from a separate store (perhaps outside) before and after a morning's play. In response to changing social patterns, some play-groups now offer considerably extended hours to cover the childcare needs of employed parents, rather than the original two mornings a week. With children possibly spending as much as eight hours a day in play-groups, for perhaps five days a week, the question of their physical sur-roundings becomes much more significant. There remains considerable work to be done to raise the standards of many preschools, most notably in terms of the actual accommodation and suitable outside play areas, and in improving the qualifications of the staff.

2. Children's centres

Ages of children: 0–5 (may also offer after-school care)
Opening times: weekdays throughout the year

UNIVERSITY OF WINCHESTER
LIBRARY

The new concept of the children's centre has evolved from previous Early Excellence and family centres, first mentioned in official legislation in the 1989 Children Act, though some had been in existence at least ten years earlier. Originally some were community-run, but many others were set up and funded (sometimes in partnership with the local authority) by existing voluntary organisations, particularly the Save the Children Fund (SCF), Barnardos and the NCH Action for Children. The intention of these early family centres was to offer a varied and flexible set of activities to both children and adults, especially in disadvantaged localities.

The new children's centres, some of which are called Sure Start children's centres, have become a central feature in the new early years landscape. At the time of writing they offer a diverse set of services. Some cater for full-time care and education while others have more informal activities including 'drop-in' sessions (for any parents with or without their children), 'special needs' groups, toy libraries, adult education and ante-natal clinics. The plan is to provide a comprehensive universal service across England with children's centres based in every community – in other words a 'one-stop shop' incorporating high-quality nursery education, some day care for the children of working parents, integrated health and social care, and advice for parents, all within an ethos of partnership with parents.

The challenge of finding appropriately trained staff, especially the right person to be in charge of these multi-agency children's centres, remains formidable. Until very recently there was no directly suitable qualification that covered all the specialised knowledge and skills required for work in at least three 'dimensions', i.e. with children, with parents, and also with the community at large. Ideally a very broad-based inter-disciplinary preparation is necessary. In 2006, therefore, a pioneering National Professional Qualification in Integrated Centre Leadership (NPQICL) was launched. Although this is now available nationally, and is being taken up in large numbers, it will be some time until all leaders are properly trained. The vision of centres with an integrated workforce is admirable but there are many issues left outstanding. One serious remaining problem is the unequal status and resulting pay differential within the staff team.

3. Private nurseries

Ages of children: 0–5 years
Opening times: weekdays throughout the year

The private nursery offering all-day care and education is something of a growth industry, yet the demand for facilities caring for babies up to school age is still far from being met. Business firms (such as banks), institutions (such as colleges, universities and hospitals), national commercial nursery chains and private individuals are among those who offer such services. They operate under all sorts of titles and names – crèches, kindergartens, nurseries, 'Tiny Tots', 'Caterpillars' or whatever is fancied. Some are set up with an eye to profits, but if the provision is good and the staff properly recompensed, and the cost reasonable for parents, nurseries are not moneyspinners. The private enterprise nurseries vary extremely in quality. If some are excellent, others barely meet the criteria laid down by Ofsted. Good-quality staff are hard to find, the result being that young (often very young) women with limited training are taken on. Pay is low, a factor in the very high turnover of staff. Far more training, especially in work with babies and toddlers, is needed for personnel in these settings. Since parents are generally out working it is hardly surprising that few of them are actually involved. Because private nurseries are inevitably expensive they tend to be used by people earning reasonably high salaries rather than by the unemployed or poorer members of society.

4. Independent private schools

Ages of children: 3- and 4-year-olds
Opening times: school terms and school hours

A small but growing number of children attend private nursery schools or classes, which are invariably linked to independent preparatory or pre-preparatory schools. Generally the class sizes are quite small. It is interesting to note that anyone can legally set up a 'school' and employ 'teachers' who are not actually qualified as such, but the schools must at least now conform to Ofsted's regulations. Parents will almost certainly find these schools an expensive option since they are often run for profit.

5. Nursery schools and classes

Ages of children: 3– and 4– year-olds
Opening times: school terms and school hours; most children attend half-time

A nursery *school* is a self-contained establishment catering for children of preschool age unlike a nursery *class* attached to an infant or primary school. Originally the responsibility of local education authorities, both of these educational facilities are unevenly distributed countrywide. In some cities there are enough places for virtually every child to attend, whereas rural counties tend to provide very few or indeed no nursery schools or classes at all. Because they have always been part of the school system, nursery schools and classes are required to be in the charge of a fully trained teacher who must have either a four-year BEd degree or a three-year degree followed by a PGCE (Postgraduate Certificate of Education). Along with the teacher each class will have one or two qualified nursery assistants. Three- and four-year-olds attend these types of pre-school, at no cost to parents but almost always only for half days – indeed, the morning or afternoon session may be quite brief, perhaps as little as two hours. Considering this limited provision, and given the length of school holidays, these establishments are far from meeting the needs of working parents.

Traditional British nursery schools have nonetheless merited an international reputation for excellence and been an influential model in the development of preschool curricula around the world. Their philosophy is distinctive and grounded on the creation of a well-endowed, carefully planned environment in which all the children are given personal responsibility to choose their own activities supported by well-informed and sensitive adults. The child's all-round development is the ultimate goal, but the underlying belief is that children can fulfil their potential through the powerful force of their individual intrinsic motivation. The nursery teacher and assistant are trained in how to provide stimulating and challenging play activities through which children's learning takes place. *Just Playing?* (Moyles 1989) gives a lucid account of education through play in the classroom.

Over the last few years some nursery schools have changed their status and become Family Centres, Early Excellence Centres, and eventually new children's centres as described earlier. Among early years professionals there is some regret that the kind of ethos once associated with nursery schools seems to have been diluted and changed as the government's concept of 'early education' is rolled out across every type of setting.

6. Parent and toddler groups

Ages of children: 0–5 years
Opening times: one or two sessions (2 hours) per week usually in term times

These are very informal groups, not normally regulated in any official way since parents remain with their children all the time. On account of the lack of registration the number of parent and toddler (P/T) groups is unknown, but they are ubiquitous. Their aim is to create a haven where the adults can make social contacts and the children play with others in relaxed surroundings. All kinds of people besides parents make use of P/T groups, including childminders and nannies. This mutual support may in fact be enormously helpful to more isolated carers of young children and for those at risk of depression. The majority of children who attend are under three (after this age they usually 'graduate' to playgroups where they stay without their parents). Some mothers even attend P/T groups before their babies are born. It is common for P/T groups to share the same premises as preschools (church and village halls, for example), and some may even share equipment. The responsibility for running the P/T group is shouldered by volunteer helpers, and parents pay a small fee to cover the costs of the rent, heat, refreshments and other consumables. The number of adults and children present in the group at any session is very variable – from say, three or four parents with a total of perhaps four children, up to groups with ten times that number.

7. Childminders

Ages of children: 0 upwards
Opening times: full day throughout the year

Childminder care is often the arrangement chosen for babies and children under two, and indeed this may be the only solution open to parents because of the lack of group provision for under-twos. But even when group care is available, some families may prefer the option of childminding. Not only does it offer a home-like atmosphere, but the small numbers of children present allow for more individual care as well as potentially more flexible personal arrangements for the parents. Child-minders are required by law to be registered with Ofsted if they are caring for a child (to whom they are not related) 'for reward' for more than two hours a day. There is concern that there may still be some childminders working unregistered. In assessing whether a childminder is suitable for registration, the quality of the person as well as the environment (health and safety, and available play equipment) is taken into consideration.

Childminding has had a poor press in the past, and occasional examples of bad practice do still occur, but where it is good it can be very good indeed. The National Childminding Association (NCMA) has played a vital role in raising the status and practice of childminders. Local support groups and training have given these potentially isolated workers the kind of backing, information and increased understanding of child development they need. There is still some way to go in ensuring that services such as 'drop-in' centres, support groups and training groups are accessible to all minders. Childminders must not feel cut off. The final point to emphasise is an economic one. Childminding is not cheap to parents, but on the other hand, childminders deserve a realistic wage.

CHAPTER SEVEN

Observation and Assessment

The word 'assessment' is becoming ever more frequently used in all UK services for children. So common is the word that most people will immediately think that they know what is meant. In fact, though, it is a tricky word meaning different things to different people.

Each profession has traditionally defined assessment largely in its own way, as will be discussed later in this chapter following a brief introduction. For teachers the National Curriculum and associated Standardised Assessment Tasks (SATS) govern the nature of assessment, fixing their attention clearly on every child's educational attainment. The *Early Years Foundation Stage* (EYFS), now in place for every child and every setting (including childminding), specifically links observation and assessment. For social workers, on the other hand, the concept of assessment is particularly devoted to children with social needs whose family circumstances are in question. Here assessment is about assembling information on children's all-round development and their problems in the family context. By contrast again, health workers in their medical context generally adopt the word 'assessment' in association with the monitoring of a child's physical progress. While these various interpretations of the nature of assessment overlap to some extent, the emphasis differs according to each profession. Now, however, following the changes to the structure of children's services noted in Chapter One, a common approach is required, since the new *Common Assessment Framework* (CAF) charges the whole interdisciplinary team of professionals to work together in the assessment of children in need. This chapter explores the ideas around assessment further, considers the relationship between observation and assessment in various professional areas, and touches on some practical aspects in utilising the CAF.

The methods that professionals rely on for making assessments range from the very controlled and structured to the unintrusive and open-ended. Observation is one of the basic tools for assessment, coming at the informal end of the continuum. It probably contributes to most other assessment procedures too.

This book has stressed throughout the importance of seeing what children are actually doing and hearing what they are actually saying, avoiding as far as possible preconceptions as to what this might, or should, be. One might say that through observation we are searching for the 'real' child. To search in this way demands keeping an open and receptive state of mind as well as an ability to record (mentally and on paper) the fine detail of a child's behaviour – attitudes and skills which may have to be acquired. Non-interpretative, non-judgemental *observation* thus stands in sharp contrast to *assessment*, which is all about weighing up and measuring progress, making judgements about what has been learned, interpreting behaviour and making decisions. Assessments are supposed to be valid, objective and unambiguous. But we should not ignore the part played in assessment-making by personal expectations, preconceived attitudes towards children, cultural values, legal constraints and professional priorities. All these are inevitably present. No assessment can actually be purely objective and clinical. This problematic area is difficult to handle because such expectations, attitudes and values are often unconsciously held, and questioning deeply rooted beliefs can be uncomfortable and unsettling. In assessing children the problem must nevertheless be confronted. People who work with children will particularly need to consider their personal concepts of childhood, their understanding of children's rights, their attitudes to parents' own views about bringing up children, and the cultural context in which they are working. They need to be conscious too of the narrowing effect of professional theory and practice, which may channel thinking and perhaps constrict it. As has been seen in Chapter Two, *Views on Children and Childhood*, there are many different standpoints.

When the New Zealand Ministry of Education introduced the Te Whaariki curriculum for the early years in the 1990s it occasioned much debate regarding what form of assessment to use across all settings in that country. This curriculum was based on 'strands of learning outcome' – well-being, belonging, communication, contribution and exploration. But it could not be measured against the previously used assessment schedules that described children's progress in terms of physical, intellectual, emotional and social skills and understandings, since these took the form of checklists using a 'deficit model' (designed to find the gaps in children's progress rather than discovering what they could do). The new Te Whaariki model of assessment concentrated on 'learning stories', i.e. observed evidence of what children were actually doing and expressing. This in turn was analysed according to learning dispositions such as the child's willingness to be involved. (This perspective is discussed further in Chapter Five, in the section on concentration and involvement. For a full account of New Zealand's form of assessment in early education see Carr 2001.)

While adults working in children's services can generally be assumed to have altruistic motives for their choice of profession, they probably rarely consider the power that they wield, especially in the case of health and social workers whose ordinary everyday actions can have far-reaching consequences. All the same they may feel relatively power-less given the strong system of regulations they must now comply with. They also suffer from the media spotlight shone on any case that appears to demonstrate mistakes or misjudgements. Practical training sessions for groups of adults, either in the workplace or on courses, would raise awareness about the issues of rights, responsibilities and power included the 1989 UN Convention on The Rights of The Child. However, profes-sional training nowadays, in the light of *Every Child Matters* and all the related legislation, will as a rule lay more stress on meeting government requirements rather than the more subtle complications of power rela-tionships.

Personal subjectivity cannot be escaped when making assessments. Moreover, professional habit also influences observations and, in turn, assessments. The way that professional assumptions can shape judg-ements is nicely illustrated in this medical example. A radiologist's report on the X-rays of a child with a persistent cough concluded that there was no apparent reason for the problem. However, a second radiograph revealed a button in the child's throat. The button was removed and the cough stopped. The first X-ray was re-examined and the button was visible there too. The radiologist had too easily assumed that the child was wearing a vest with a button at the neck. Dr Jane Abercombie, who used this case on training courses, pointed out that 'persistent, deep-rooted and well-organised classifications of ways of thinking and behaving' are always shaping our interpretations of situations or data (quoted in Drummond 1993, p.79).

Given that multi-disciplinary teams are now working together, there is a much greater need for discussion about the various values held by colleagues from different professional backgrounds, preferably before dealing with actual cases. (The complex issues of multi-disciplinary working are examined in two recent books, Anning *et al.* 2006 and Siraj-Blatchford 2007.) In the light of these warnings about the dangers of subjectivity, bias, professional expectations, culture-bound perceptions and so on, it is helpful to set down guiding principles for all workers making assessments about young children. The insistence of the 1989 Children Act that the interests of the child are paramount is as relevant as ever and is maintained by later legislation based on *Every Child Matters*. Children must be respected as individuals with their own ideas, experiences, achievements and backgrounds – cultural, religious or whatever. Any assessment should not only recognise different learning and personal needs, it should equally take account of the child's opinions. Parents (or those standing in for them) must have a voice too. A reciprocal exchange of information with parents should always be incorporated into assessment arrangements when major decisions are being made. (Readers will find more extensive discussions about the principles of assessment in Drummond 1993.)

The concept of assessment

Assessment in children's services has many purposes. It helps professionals to understand children as individuals, to monitor their progress, and to identify those children at risk or with special needs. Assessment also enables staff to evaluate the services they offer and informs curriculum planning (activities, materials and organisational arrangements). Furthermore it generates information that can be communicated to other professionals and parents. As far as education goes, Nutbrown (2006a) identifies three broad purposes of assessment:

- assessment for teaching and learning
- assessment for management and accountability
- assessment for research.

In the next section five different styles of assessment are explored – formative, diagnostic, summative, evaluative and informative. The actual form of assessment will vary according to its intended function. The new EYFS profile requires very specific forms of assessment covering all aspects of learning and development and sets down the lists of 'standards' in very great detail. We should note, though, that other European countries do not use this prescriptive approach, and neither do Scotland and Wales.

Formative assessment

Formative assessment describes the normal method of keeping track of an individual child's progress since it is an on-going procedure and serves to illuminate such areas as learning, feelings and social relationships. Informed by this type of assessment adults are in a better position to understand the child and to plan appropriately. For instance, with increased awareness they may be able to judge whether the child is on the brink of a new phase of development, the 'zone of proximal development' as it was called by Vygotsky (see Chapter Two). Children learn most effectively and easily if adults are able to recognise and capitalise on this kind of 'readiness'. Formative assessment also aids planning for the whole group of children.

Diagnostic assessment

Diagnostic assessment is self-explanatory. It allows adults to identify possible barriers to progress (e.g. deafness, dyslexia, hyperactivity), where, for instance, a child may need special help or particular targeted activities. The importance of the early years as a time for discovering special needs can hardly be over-emphasised. Diagnostic assessment based on observation spans all child-oriented services and professions. The sensitive awareness and observations of staff may alert them to behaviour or symptoms that point to current problems in children's lives such as neglect or abuse (physical, emotional or sexual). When there are doubts on any score then staff will of course be expected to act quickly, making contact with appropriate local authority officers or other organisations.

Summative assessment

Another type of assessment is summative, which comes at the conclusion of a term or a year or other period. It *sums up* the progress and learning that have taken place. Final examinations at school and university are of this type, and so too are the Standardised Assessment Tasks (SATS). The intention behind SATS is to tell teachers and parents what the children have achieved according to the kind of measure (in this case a test) that has been applied. Such information does not, however, offer much insight into how children are thinking, nor can it shed any light on areas of learning other than those actually being examined. An associated problem is that the pressure of testing may profoundly influence what is actually taught. Indeed, examples of 'teaching to the test' crop up every year. Hence, there is a serious cause for concern that, because a defined curriculum is laid down, children's actual learning experiences can be constrained. Whole areas, notably the arts in general, have been effectively downplayed at the expense of what are deemed more 'basic' subjects. Interestingly the government has now come to recognise this imbalance and is promoting various initiatives to improve access to the marginalised creative areas of experience. The nub of the problem, however, is that while the testing regime remains in place, these initiatives will usually have limited effect.

Acceptable as an approach for older children, summative assessment is less relevant to the early years than other kinds of assessment. It frequently involves a test-type situation inappropriate for young children who are so intensely curious that they are very easily distracted by something that looks more interesting. As a result they may well not concentrate on the test or task they are set or may become fascinated by some irrelevant aspect. They are in addition very sensitive to the social context. Their ease with people they know often belies their wariness and shyness with an unfamiliar person, but even a known adult behaving in an unfamiliar manner can be disconcerting. Even though the testing at the age of seven attempts to be informal, the atmosphere of the tests has a formality that is inappropriate to young children. Moreover children's interpretation of the circumstances of the test influences their response. Donaldson (1978) and Tizard and Hughes (1984) have described the variations in children's understanding of and reaction to situations. In a classic example, Margaret Donaldson once explored children's thinking as they carried out Piagetian tasks. Her imaginative re-design of these tasks and her attention to children's knowledge of context cast doubt on their universal validity and helped change views about children's stages of understanding. In one case, in order to evaluate children's recognition of space and perspective, a particular task involved a boy trying to hide behind model cardboard walls so that an imaginary policeman could not see him. This was an improvement on Piaget's Swiss original, which depended on the visibility of mountains behind various other hills, but failed to allow for the likelihood that not all children would be familiar with mountain landscapes in the way most Swiss children are.

Evaluative assessment

Evaluative assessment is not so much centred on a single child, even though observation of individual children will still contribute to this kind of assessment. The reason for evaluation is to 'weigh up' the quality of what is being offered in terms of equipment, activities, the contributions of the staff, and the environment in general. Sometimes the word 'review' is preferred instead. One Time Sampling example given earlier (in Chapter Four) paid attention to the use of the book corner, and information recorded in this sort of observation might serve in evaluation. Which children were visiting the book corner? How often? And what were they actually doing there? Such evidence might indicate that the book corner should be re-designed – perhaps a reorganisation of the space and a better choice of books.

Informative assessment

Drummond (1993) included one other type of assessment, which she labelled informative and which specially concerns the reciprocal sharing of information about children between parents and preschool staff. This matters, because parents are the first 'educators' of their children, and early years staff should always regard them as partners. All services for young children support the idea of partnership with parents and try to achieve it, but with varying degrees of intensity and success. Partnership is a broad concept and the comments that follow deal solely with the sharing of information in that relationship. Since parents want (and have a right) to know how their child is getting on, preschool staff need ways of collecting and communicating this information – in other words they require a record-keeping system. When developing an effective system several kinds of system are worth consideringing. Whichever one is chosen it must be easy to use and understood by other professionals and parents alike; it must be precise yet quick to complete; and the information it brings together must be as factual as possible.

Many different record-keeping systems can be found in operation. Most will now relate to the EYFS profile, though in addition some preschools maintain a portfolio (or file) for each child in which are placed items selected by either the child or the adults. Typical portfolios would include drawings, paintings, perhaps photographs and other two-dimensional work, and observations by the staff. Material from informative assessments may be passed on to the next preschool setting or to school.

As children enter the reception class of statutory schooling they will probably be assessed in several areas of the EYFS profile, namely personal, social and emotional development, communication, language and literacy, and numeracy attainment. The reason for this is to provide a baseline against which later achievements can be measured. Assessment at this stage must be regarded as controversial and can be criticised using the arguments that might be deployed against any preschool testing. Certainly it is a pity that teachers are required to spend time administering such assessments – time that could be better spent in more direct activity with children. All the same, teachers and local education authorities are obliged (at the time of writing) to carry out these assessments in order to safeguard themselves from criticism. And at least it allows them to demonstrate in some fashion what the children were capable of on entry to school when compared with their achievement at the age of seven in Key Stage 1 testing. This is just one example, though, of the way that testing can drive teaching practice.

Assessment issues in integrated services

The relatively new *Common Assessment Framework* (CAF) supplies the format for all children's services, and every involved professional is expected to contribute to it. In practice this means that teachers, childminders, health visitors, social care workers, doctors and so on could all be part of an assessment. These integrated services expect fresh styles of collaboration between different professionals, voluntary organisations and parents. It follows that all concerned must be quite clear about the meaning of key words. When talking with colleagues within our own professional group we use jargon and linguistic short-cuts. There is nothing wrong with this since it speeds up communication. In *inter-disciplinary* working however, dialogue must necessarily be at a more explicit level and free from possible ambiguities. Discussion about terminology is in fact often rewarding and revealing for it helps to clarify personal understanding. As pointed out already 'assessment' is one of these key words that needs using with precision. Since it has various shades of meaning it may benefit from an accompanying adjective, such as 'diagnostic' or 'normative'.

In social work the term is most commonly employed at the stage when a range of information is brought together for the purpose of drawing up plans for a child's future. But there is a prior stage when the term might also be found, namely at the warning and referral level. Observation is a very important tool at this point. An alert, well-trained social worker will be able to recognise signs that children's physical or mental health and development are being impaired as a consequence of the care (or lack of it) they are receiving. The next step – carrying out the intervention strategies – will also involve careful observation of the child. Following on from this, social workers will evaluate the outcomes of those strategies – at which stage highly skilled observation will again come into play.

Besides recognising health and development problems, social workers (and indeed all who work with young children) will be on the lookout for symptoms that might indicate stress, neglect or abuse. Some of these have already been mentioned but they bear repeating. Professionals should always take special heed of children who seem withdrawn, 'frozen' or excessively watchful; who appear miserable and anxious and unable to enjoy themselves; who are hostile and behave angrily; who have a very low tolerance of frustration or failure (judged according to their age); who cannot cope with new situations; who have poor relationships with other children and adults; and who exhibit low self-esteem. As the case of Victoria Climbié demonstrated (Laming 2003), social workers working with cultures different from their own face a special challenge.

The CAF form provides a complex and very extensive list of questions to answer under the headings of 'development', 'parents and carers' and 'family and environmental'. Commendably this does reflect the essential holistic and ecological perspectives. In order to respond to all these questions, however, professionals will need to have observed children in great detail, and preferably in more than one situation. Take one of the CAF criteria under 'development', that of 'behaviour development'. Here the key indicators are stated to be: self-control, reckless or impulsive behaviour, restless and over-active behaviour, easily distracted behaviour, short attention span and poor concentration. Now imagine various scenarios – an average preschool environment in a free play situation, a child's own home where there are 'controlling' parents, an after-school club, or a centre for children under care orders (where they meet the parent they are not living with). A child is likely to behave differently in each case. In the last situation, a centre for children under care orders, children have been observed to behave and talk in completely different ways with the parents they are and are not living with, and differently again in one-to-one conversations with their social worker.

In another example from the CAF criteria under 'development', that of 'learning', the key indicators involve 'understanding, reasoning and problem-solving, organising, making connections, being creative, exploring, experimenting, imaginative play, interaction, participation in learning, aspirations, motivation and perseverance' (*Every Child Matters* CAF form, p.5). One might expect class teachers to have paid attention to some of these qualities, but the research of 5x5x5=creativity, an arts-based educational project (see Chapters Nine and Ten), has shown that they often do not. Many teachers involved in this project have been amazed at the unsuspected creativity of children in their encounters with artists. When children had the freedom to express themselves through play and the 'hundred languages' (also see Chapter Ten) they demonstrated capacities and characteristics never observed in the ordinary daily classroom routine. In the 5x5x5 example of Tommy, teachers explicitly commented that they were unaware of this child's depth of feeling, and would never have discerned it in normal everyday practice.

In all work with children, whether at the early stage of recognising that a child may be 'in need' or 'at risk', at the investigative stage of gathering further data for the CAF, during the assessment of the case leading to decision-making, and in the later phases of reviewing and monitoring progress, observation will almost always play a part. At every stage the skilled observer will take time to watch and listen, to remain calm and thoughtful and, most important, to avoid rushing to conclusions too rapidly. However, as has been shown, assessment is not as straightforward a concept as is often assumed.

CHAPTER EIGHT

Supporting Child Observation

This chapter primarily addresses lecturers, organisers and trainers designing course programmes that include the topic of child observation. It is organised into three sections: the first section sets out the background, the second identifies the learning objectives for course programmes and covers key issues in observation, while the third section suggests some strategies for teaching observation through lectures and seminars, observation sessions, and evaluation and assessment.

Background

The *Every Child Matters* (ECM) agenda now provides the context for all professionals (see Chapter One) and to supplement it the government has produced a stream of related documents. Three of these – *Care Matters: Time for change* (DCSF 2007a), the *Common Assessment Framework* (DCSF 2005) and *The Children's Plan* (DCSF 2007) – all ask initial training courses and continuing professional development to pay special attention to observation. Another publication, *Every Child Matters, Change for Children* (Department for Education and Skills 2005), sets out six areas of expertise under the 'Common Core of Skills and Knowledge':

- promoting effective communication and engagement
- promoting child and young person development
- safeguarding and promoting the welfare of the child
- supporting transitions
- working in a multi-agency mode
- sharing information.

UNIVERSITY OF WINCHESTER
LIBRARY

Observation is clearly seen as a 'building block' underlying all these areas. It is an essential element in communication skills, where the official guidance defines communication as involving words, body language and effectiveness in listening. Under the heading *Child and young person development* the whole process starts with observation leading to decision-making (see Chapter Seven on assessment). The EYFS, now the statutory requirement for all young children's services, depends on a philosophy of personalised learning which must inevitably depend on observation. *The Children's Plan* (DCSF 2007b) in its priorities states that: 'The best settings carry out observation as part of their day-to-day work. However, high quality observation and assessment are far from universally used, and as a result children can miss out on the help they need from adults' (Section 3.35).

Integrated working in children's services is now assumed and this chapter has multi-disciplinary application – though with some bias towards the training of social workers. It should be noted that this book as a whole provides relevant and significant material applicable to the new qualification for children's social workers where 'social pedagogy' is central. Social pedagogy, while common across Europe where it is a separate professional group, is not well known in the UK. The new course at the Thomas Coram Research Unit with the title *Pedagogy – a holistic, personal approach to work with children and young people across services* indicates the nature of the concept.

With major changes throughout children's services still being embedded, concern has been expressed that initial and in-service professional development is still far from adequate. One factor in these deficiencies is a serious shortage of tutors with the specialist skills required for preparing students – actually a long-standing problem.

Learning objectives

The SCIE (Social Care Institute for Excellence) Knowledge Review of 'Teaching and Learning and Assessing Communication Skills in Social Work Education' (Luckock *et al.* 2006) found disturbing evidence of a lack of preparation for communication skills, inadequate attention paid to the 'nature' of childhood, and uncertainty about the aims of courses. In consequence, learning objectives for students have not been strictly defined or properly integrated. The review found variations on emphasis. Some courses stressed the therapeutic aspects of communication and the implications of empathy towards the families and children in professional care, while others concentrated on teaching information and technical skills. In fact both approaches are necessary. Lecturers intending to introduce planned child observation as a component of communication skills, on both pre-service training and post-qualifying programmes, will need to be fully convinced about the value of such sessions. The pressures of an already overcrowded syllabus and the notion that child observation is a worthy but minority interest may have to be resisted.

Chapter One of this book explained why observation matters and covered the rationale in some detail. These ideas determine the learning objectives for courses or single units. By the end of a course programme the following topics will have been covered and the students should:

- understand the purposes and methods of several observation techniques

- be able to put one or two methods into practice using communication and planning skills

- have analysed and reflected on the observations and the views of children they observed

- have evaluated the processes involved

- have examined their own personal learning and its effect on their own emotions, both in the observational study and as regards the implications for future practice.

Observation as a technique and mode of behaviour

Students should have the opportunity to compare different techniques. Chapter Four shows how totally different data may be collected using different methods, each having its distinctive merits and limitations. Learning how to make observational records is to a large extent a matter of skill development, and therefore needs practice, but it also requires a clear understanding of the observer's 'stance' in relation to the children and their families.

The skills of observation contrast markedly with the more active intervention that is characteristic of social workers, educators, health workers and indeed all professionals in their encounters with children. Students need to be initiated into this seemingly passive mode of behaviour, which they may feel is almost unnatural. They must learn how to maintain a heightened state of attention in which they see and absorb all that they can. Danielle Turney (2008) writes about understanding the 'observer stance' – a kind of 'detached engagement' in which the observer is aware of the whole milieu and its dynamics. Close non-judgemental observation is the only agenda. For now, decisions about the child should be deferred, especially in the case of social workers still absorbed in the observation process.

Uncertainty in observation

Students need help in accepting this special observer role, in which they may feel tense and somehow de-skilled. 'Allowing oneself to become properly aware of the child's unconscious communications…may seem impossible for an inexperienced, over-stretched and possibly frightened [social] worker' (Turney 2008, p.123) – a statement that may apply to others too when observing children. Although student observers are technically non-participant in that they are not in a planning or interventionist role, their position is still somewhat ambiguous. In fact Elfer and Selleck (1999), quoting from the work of the Tavistock Institute, conclude that: 'observers are unavoidably *participant* observers to a certain degree, however passive and non-interventionist a role they try to take' (Rustin 1989, p.61). Further they note human beings empathise with the feelings of others, even when these are not expressed in words. Elfer and Selleck note that 'the stereotypical example of a baby crying in the supermarket, [makes] those around him or her feel desperate, or anxious or just relieved this baby is not their baby' (p.72). A child's expression of strong feelings may in turn evoke emotions in the observer, especially when the latter is torn between whether to intervene or not.

> 'to be a good observer…requires a space in the mind where thoughts can begin to take shape and where confused experiences can be held in an inchoate form until their meaning becomes clearer. This kind of mental functioning requires a capacity to tolerate anxiety, uncertainty, discomfort, helplessness, a sense of bombardment.' (Rustin 1989, pp.20–21).

The SCIE study referred to above also draws attention to another cause of uncertainty and unease for social work students. A growing acceptance of children as capable, intentional and self-determining can clash with the concept of children as vulnerable beings in need of care and protection.

Other issues affecting observation

Student observers should be alive to the dangers of discrimination. They must recognise possible prejudices in themselves and possibly in their profession that lead to stereotyping. With regard to meeting the specific needs of ethnic minority and mixed parentage children Dwivedi's helpful book on this subject (2002) points out that professionals rarely search out the 'story' of the child or parent. In this regard observations should properly take a narrative form without abstract reasoning. As always the most important focus is the actual child.

Children's rights and points of view equally need acknowledging. Baldwin (1994) was concerned that observation (at least in social work training) may get hived off as a separate skill. 'In their observations students need to do more than note difference. They need to be able to note the hierarchy of culture and consequent oppression. They need in their analyses to use that understanding to inform their practice' (p.80).

Studying child development should clearly entail the observation of individual children. All students preparing to work with children ought to be familiar in advance with the main stages of development, and this knowledge should be brought together in a holistic and 'ecological' view of the child's growth, as explained in Chapter Three. Observational work likewise provides students with an opportunity to consider how they might draw on their own past experiences as they discover children's lives.

Finally, general observational skills are transferable across many professional settings and apply to all age ranges, though certain skills and knowledge relate more specifically to children than to adults. In the wider perspective the reflective approach advocated by Schön (1987) could equally be integrated into preparatory professional training as a whole. He has been critical of the mechanistic and overly rational style of much training in all professions.

Teaching observation skills

Though there will be a need for introductory lectures, seminars and discussions, the skills of observation will be best developed through experiential learning on the job. The following pattern is suggested: an introductory lecture, preparatory activities in small seminar groups, a series of observational visits, and then further seminars at which students analyse their observations and discuss issues of special interest or concern.

The preparatory lecture discussing the rationale of observation should also introduce students to some of the possible recording strategies (set out in Chapter Four). Seminar work will allow experimentation with these methods and discovery of their possibilities. The material for these activities can be either brief video sequences or simple, short, role plays. Almost any section of a video showing children interacting might be used, though one with a distracting voice-over commentary is not recommended. By having the whole group watch a sequence together, recording what they have observed, several other topics will no doubt arise in addition to debate about the recording method itself.

One significant topic to highlight during these sessions is that of subjectivity. Even experienced professionals are often less objective, dispassionate and distanced than they assume. Activities that heighten students' awareness of this danger are valuable at this stage. For example, it is worthwhile 'engineering' a discrepancy of opinions about a witnessed event in a seminar to make a point vividly. Students might thus be shown a section of video *after* being primed with different information in advance. One half of the group might be told (without the others hearing) that they are about to see an ordinary family scene, while the rest are informed that there is a suspicion of abuse in the family. In the subsequent discussion, perceptions of the two groups are likely to be strikingly at odds. Students' interpretations and feelings about behaviour may relate back to their own childhood. Small group discussions in which students recall childhood family rules, for example, might raise these issues. Another technique that has proved very revealing is getting the students in seminar groups to recall occasions of unfairness in their childhood.

Outside the planned observation task, students may be able to visit each other on placement in order to compare their immediate impressions *as a visitor* with the perceptions of the student on the spot who has become familiar with the scene and atmosphere.

In addition to the inevitable subjectivity of observation, the question of selectivity also comes up in recording what is observed. Everything cannot be written down; choices must be made. This can be demonstrated by getting students to compare their individual notes on a shared observation in a seminar. A similar activity may further sharpen students' interest in the effects of memory, selectivity and subjectivity. A short role play, involving, say, two students, could be set up and staged. The rest of the group observe and then write an account from memory, describing what took place, why the actors reacted as they did in their roles, how they interpreted the responses of the other participants, and finally what in retrospect they learned from the episode emotionally and otherwise. The descriptions can then be compared.

The issue of stereotyping on the basis of class, culture, race, gender, sexual orientation and disability should be reviewed at this stage, before the actual observations take place. This is covered in detail in Chapter Four. One further problem of recording concerns the actual use of words. Students might be given practice exercises that involve comparisons of the vocabulary used. They must learn to use *descriptive* language, not *judgemental* or *interpretative* language, in the actual record. For example:

Descriptive: 'Places bricks on table noisily'

Judgemental: 'Places bricks on table in an angry manner'

Interpretative: 'Shows he's tired and in a bad mood today as he places bricks on table'.

Preparation for a child study involves helping students select a child for observation. When such an observational study is part of a social work placement, it is unwise to choose a child already identified as needing special intervention, for this raises ethical issues. When vulnerable children are under watch, close scrutiny by a student observer might seem intrusive, tactless and even harmful, placing additional strain on children 'at risk', 'in need' or facing other difficulties in their lives. Furthermore it is better for students not to be involved in the continuing assessment procedures surrounding such children, but to concentrate entirely on learning the skills of observation.

Staff at the setting will often suggest a particular child as a subject of an observation, but it is always worth considering why that proposal was made – perhaps she is a 'star' child, or else one causing some concern, or even a child whose parents are known to be especially amenable to such a study. One student mistakenly complained that the child he had been asked to observe was unsuitable for observation because he was only 18 months old and not yet talking – and so offered him little to write down. This of course represented a false view of very young children as somehow not competent thinkers and unable to communicate in alternative ways.

The actual setting up of the observational visits might seem time-consuming, but it will be time well spent. Students should always select a child who is unknown to them (another reason for students on social work placement not to choose one of their client cases). It is best to do this by making direct contact with a local preschool or perhaps a Sure Start Children's Centre (for more information about settings see Chapter Six). Most students seem to find a convenient preschool group without much difficulty, but it would certainly be helpful for the tutor to compile a list of local groups that have been welcoming in the past and to make this available to students. The actual task of investigating local preschool services and talking to staff is a relevant exercise in its own right and in relation to future social work practice. Of course students require a letter of introduction from the university or college explaining the nature of the child study observations, why the student has been asked to do them, how many visits he or she will make, and what is expected of the pre-school staff. (A more detailed account of the process of making contact, negotiating the arrangement and obtaining children's consent will be found in Chapter Four.) At the planning stage lecturers should also advise students what to do if they observe situations that seem dangerous or damaging to children. A student observer would normally intervene only if a child was in imminent physical danger. However, students may spot other worrying aspects of a setting, such as apparently poor child care, racist and sexist attitudes, or other signs of discrimination. Though inappropriate to raise with the staff the student should discuss worries with his or her tutor as soon as possible.

Observers' childhood memories

As already mentioned, observation often triggers powerful emotions, perhaps relating to the observer's childhood. At the start of the preparatory seminars it is advisable to remind the students of the support systems they have access to in their own institution for counselling, tutorial support and more specific support networks. The matter of privacy versus self-disclosure might be aired at this stage so that members of the seminar group can control the extent to which they share their past or present feelings. In any case, the purpose of the seminars is the development of observation skills; it is not a forum for counselling.

Reflective discussions

Once the observational visits are under way, seminar groups are valuable for support as well as for discussing and reflecting on the issues arising from the observations. Student presentations of their observations offer good opportunities for practising the descriptive narrative language necessary to communicate clear detailed accounts of behaviour to their audience. There will need to be properly established ground rules regarding the confidentiality of observation. Students must at all times ensure the anonymity of their subjects.

Written assignments

Courses may prescribe some form of written assessment giving students a chance to write up their observations and link them to theoretical perspectives on childhood and development. Through their reading and lectures the students will have encountered the important theories about child development and considered them in their context of time, place and ideological approach (see Chapters Three and Five). Critical analysis of child observations in the light of different theories is potentially valuable, perhaps as a structure into which fragmentary observations may be located. Students will of course be encouraged to think independently and indeed sceptically. Should their observations seem to refute the apparent wisdom of the theory they should be encouraged to debate the matter. They may need to be reminded, of course, that they have studied only one child and should be wary of generalising from such limited evidence.

Evaluation of the observation experience

At some point tutors should encourage students to reflect on themselves as observers. The observations, once completed, can be reviewed by prompting discussion on what has been learned, and what has been enjoyed. The effect of the observational visits on all concerned should also be explored at this stage, and the last part of Chapter Four discusses this thoroughly from the points of view of various people involved: children, parents, preschool staff and the student observers.

Possible models for child observation on course programmes

For course tutors trying to incorporate child observation within course programmes, there are several other matters to resolve. Given the time pressure, the most significant issue is how best to fit into a tight schedule a meaningful series of observations and the associated seminars. What is the minimum number of observations and seminars that are practically viable and that will at the same time allow students enought time for worthwhile learning? A second difficulty lies in finding appropriate staff with the background experience necessary to lead the seminars. A third is in deciding on the relationship of any ideological frameworks (e.g. empathetic and psychoanalytical, as in the Tavistock approach) to the practicalities of observation. Many social work courses do in fact advocate the Tavistock approach, but suitably modified, since in its original form it required an extensive amount of time devoted to it – typically 15 separate hour-long observations, plus weekly seminars at which students present their observations (see Chapter Four).

To summarise the issue of timetabling, a typical observational study depends on a series of observations of a preschool child in a group setting, and in some cases one session in the child's home. The preliminary visit to a preschool is the occasion for setting up the arrangements, seeking the help of the group leader in the choice of a child for observation, and making plans for contacting the parents. Six visits on the observation itself would be the very minimum. Each observation period should last for not less than 30 minutes, preceded by some 15 minutes tuning in to the group environment. If a home visit is included, this is to help the student gain a more rounded picture of the study child's behaviour, consider the broader ecology of the child's life, and learn something of the parents' viewpoints. Tutors should always emphasise to students that home visits are not meant to be judgemental. Parents must understand that the student is interested in their child primarily for the sake of his or her studies and that all observations take place in the context of tutor guidance and with the sanction of the student's institution.

Conclusion

The observation of young children's complex and rapid development is a rich and fascinating activity and may tap into the student's own past memories. It may also teach skills for life in general. Tutors guiding students through the entire observational experience will, it is hoped, have the enthusiasm, sensitivity and knowledge to facilitate this most important part of initial training.

CHAPTER NINE

Observation, Reflection and Documentation: The Reggio Emilia Approach

Observation, reflection and documentation are all simple enough ideas but when they come together they have the potential to change the thinking of adults about the thinking of children. This chapter concentrates on an aspect of high-quality practice with children in any educational situation, whether located in preschools, schools or even hospitals.

The Reggio Emilia approach

In recent years the inspirational work of the Reggio Emilia preschools in northern Italy has had global repercussions. Their philosophical approach to young children, together with their many years of practical educational work, offers insights into the nature of children's rights and the creative potential of all children. Every school employs an artist as a full-time member of staff, not to produce 'artworks', but to nurture creative thinking in all aspects of the children's lives, in and beyond school.

Emerging from a parents' initiative towards the end of the Second World War, the preschools and infant-toddler centres of the small town of Reggio Emilia continue to develop their fine educational practice and to attract visiting educators and artists from many countries. Those first parents, in the mid-1940s, wanted schools that would encourage children to ask questions, that would see these children as citizens of their community from their earliest days, and whose staff respected the competence of even the youngest children. Loris Malaguzzi, already a young teacher, was drawn in at the very start. He proved to be the philosopher of the movement and was for many years the Director of Reggio Children, until his death in 1993.

Perhaps the main reasons for the preschools of Reggio Emilia's continuing success are:

- believing in children as capable and full of potential from the moment of birth
- accepting the role of listening adults who support and facilitate the children's own enquiries
- involving artists as partners in the educational process
- using the 'hundred languages' (a phrase from Malaguzzi's poem, in Edwards *et al.*, 1993, p.3) to communicate feelings and ideas
- creating a rich engaging environment, described as another 'teacher'
- maintaining an attitude of research and enquiry
- seeing children as social collaborators with their peers and adults
- recognising children as citizens with rights and a voice from their earliest years
- connecting at a serious level with parents and the community.

There are Reggio networks in many parts of the world. In the UK Sightlines Initiative is the reference point for Reggio Children, backed up by ReFocus groups across the country.

(For further information see http://zerosei.comune.re.it for Reggio Children in Italy and www.sightlines-initiative.com for UK information. The most comprehensive book about the Reggio approach is Edwards *et al.* 1998.)

5X5X5=creativity

In the UK a number of innovative projects have been inspired by Reggio, especially those associated with the ReFocus network under the umbrella of Sightlines Initiative, such as the Creative Foundation. Another is 5x5x5=creativity, which has established a way of working with artists in preschool settings and schools on a long-term basis. It is an arts-based educational research project and has recently become an independent charity. The name originated from the first group of five artists working with five settings in collaboration with five cultural organisations (galleries, theatres, music centres, etc.) and, since 2000, over 80 schools and settings across six local authorities (Bath and North East Somerset, Bristol, North Somerset, Somerset, Wiltshire and Oxfordshire) have taken part.

5x5x5 aims to demonstrate ways in which creativity can be fostered in and with young children through partnerships between teachers, artists and cultural organisations. Through this collaborative approach with children 5x5x5 has shown how creative activity can be at the heart of early years education. In 5x5x5 the adults see themselves as 'researching the children researching the world'. In summary the principles underlying this approach are:

- a strong belief in children as creative and competent
- ensuring a listening environment where everyone's contribution is heard
- following a creative and reflective cycle of observation, planning, action and reflection
- focusing on the process not the product
- offering many forms of expression – the concept of the hundred languages of children
- careful documentation of all activities
- continuous professional development
- collaboration with parents and the community.

(For further information see www.5x5x5creativity.org.uk, the 5x5x5 DVD *A Hundred Voices*, obtainable through the website and the book Bancroft, Fawcett and Hay 2008.) The research approach and deep thinking of both Reggio and 5x5x5 has led to a much greater understanding of children's cognitive and emotional growth.

Before examining the practical realities of this important way of working with young children we need to understand that both these approaches are guided by two highly significant principles. The first is a fundamental belief in the potential competence and creativity of all children from the moment of birth. The second concerns the collaborative process in learning.

For the educators in Reggio Emilia, social exchange is seen as essential in learning. Through shared activity, communication, cooperation, and even conflict, children co-construct their knowledge of the world, using one child's idea to develop another's, or to explore a path yet unexplored. (Gandini 1998, p.170)

Thus, social development is seen as an integral part of cognitive development.

Adhering to the two principles, the potential of children and their learning through interaction with others, it follows that a major interest for educators is in the children's explorations of their particular world and their search for meanings. Further, they aim to support children's inner drive to communicate their ideas and feelings through the many different forms of representation – poetically named in Reggio the hundred languages of children. Examples of the forms of communication that children use to share their stories, proposals, joys and fears are typically role playing, drawing, singing, dancing, making and modelling (see Chapter Ten).

In Reggio the educators and artists talk of the 'pedagogy of listening'. In other words, they develop all their teaching out of what they are learning from the children (Giudici *et al.* 2001). Their concept of the learning process thus entails adults and children enquiring together and acting as co-researchers and collaborators. Similarly the educators and artists with 5x5x5 describe their work as 'researching children researching the world' (Bancroft *et al.* 2008).

The sequential order of the three ideas in the title of this chapter – observation, reflection and documentation – matters. Chapter Four deals in detail with a range of observational methods but this chapter concentrates on observation as it relates to documentation in these two approaches, Reggio and 5x5x5.

Observation

Observations are a constant ongoing feature in both approaches. They are designed to be as open as possible, with the observer noting what actually happens, its context, and any interactions and exchanges. The processes the children and adults are using, and any diversions that may occur, are considered more important than the end results. All the adults will be participants in the gathering of observational records, and their written notes may take very different forms. Since parents as well as teaching assistants, educators and artists may all contribute observations, 5x5x5 found it best to be flexible and to allow individuals to take notes in their own personal way. The written record is of course only one possible device. Photography, video- and tape-recording, and the children's own representations – drawings, paintings, constructions and models – are all gathered. Together they reveal traces of the children's experiences. Clark and Moss (2001), using a similar framework, called it the 'Mosaic Approach' since all forms of listening to children and discovering their thinking can be used.

Example of documentation from 5x5x5: The Trap

The following example, by a parent documenter writing in an A4 blank notebook in pencil, shows the type of notes that may be collected. The setting was a primary school and the children were 4–5-year-olds from the reception classes.

CONTEXT

The school's 'quiet garden' with pathways, shrubs, nooks and crannies enabled imaginative play to take place. The artist who led the session introduced materials – card, paper, crayons, felt-tips and various other materials (big sheets of fabric, nets and string). The observational focus for the session was to identify what most fascinated the children and what developing themes were observable in their play.

Tommy: 'We need some paper. I know, let's distract them [some other children] with this drawing and we can sneak and trap them.'

Tommy has a handful of gold string. 'We can make a bird's nest with this.'

Tommy and Luke speak to each other through the tubing. Luke pulls the bushes with the string. The bushes rattle.

Luke: 'Look, I'm making the wind.' Luke ties the string around the branches.

Luke 'It's a spider's web… I'm making a trap, it's a booby trap.'

Tommy returns with some paper. 'The person who looks at this drawing is going to get trapped in Luke's trap.'

Tommy signs his name. Luke wants to make spy glasses.

Tommy: 'Now we need some string, I'll get some.'

Luke covered himself with the blue net 'Help! Help!'

Tommy: 'Who wants to get distracted by the drawings?'

Luke: 'This is good, isn't it?'

[Holly arrives on the scene.]

Holly: 'Remember, you're trapping me.'

Tommy: 'It's not ready yet. We need to take the net down to make a den.'

Reflection

This short section of observation scribed by one parent illustrates the fluid and dynamic nature of children's play. It should be noted that the observations and other materials are collected *during* the experience but that discussion and interpretations take place *later*, at the next stage. In 5x5x5 this process is described as the 'creative and reflective cycle' and is summed up in Figure 9.1.

The reflection session will involve as many of the adults who have taken part as possible. They will *revisit* the observation notes and images and share what happened from their own perspectives. In fact they may have quite different points of view about what took place, but this leads

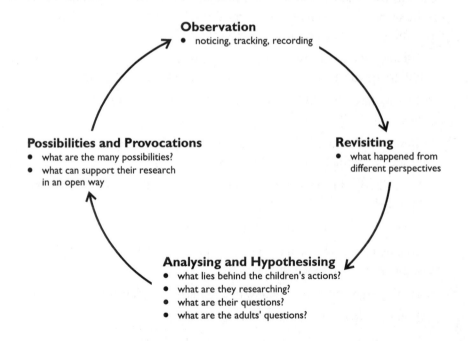

Figure 9.1: Creative and reflective cycle

into the next stage, *analysing and hypothesising.* 'What lies behind the children's actions? What were they researching? What were their questions? What are now the adults' questions?'

The next stage is to consider the *possibilities and provocations.* What are some of the deeper enquiries the children are engaged in and how might these be supported without taking over? What kinds of 'provocations' – new materials or modes (clay, paint, music, etc.), a visit, a book – would stimulate the children into deeper thinking or new enquiries?

The time given to reflection in both Reggio and 5x5x5 is prioritised and may be considered unusual. Finding the time for these sessions when other demands press in is certainly challenging. Yet reflection is absolutely central to these approaches. As long ago as 1987 Schön's research into a variety of types of professional training identified reflection as of high importance (Schön 1987). He advocated a culture in which there was reflection *in* action as well as reflection *on* action. In settings where predictability and control are so often the rule, as in some care and education institutions, he believed this flexibility and creativity were particularly needed. Adults benefit from the space to reflect on the individual child and the unpredictable situations that occur. It is interesting that Schön's research is also cited in social work literature by Briggs (1999). So much social work practice is dominated by legalistic and procedural demands that reflective practice of the kind Schön has advocated should, if at all possible, be allowed time and space. Sometimes the word 'reverie' is used to describe this reflective practice.

Documentation

Reggio employs the word 'documentation' in a special sense, as does 5x5x5. Here, documentation is not the immediate record of the observation, the rough notes, the spontaneous photographs, taped conversations, the children's drawings, and so forth but the written distillation of these records. Documentation may be described as the re-framing of the children's learning journey so that others, indeed everyone concerned including the children themselves, can then engage in what have been called the children's 'learning stories'. A learning story can be of any length, but in essence it is a summary of the sequence of the children's ideas and activities around a particular situation.

As already mentioned, when the adult participants come together to create the 'documentation' they may well find they all have different

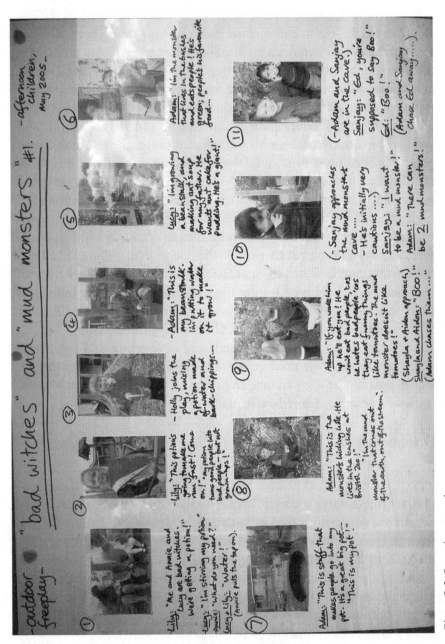

Figure 9.2: Learning story 1

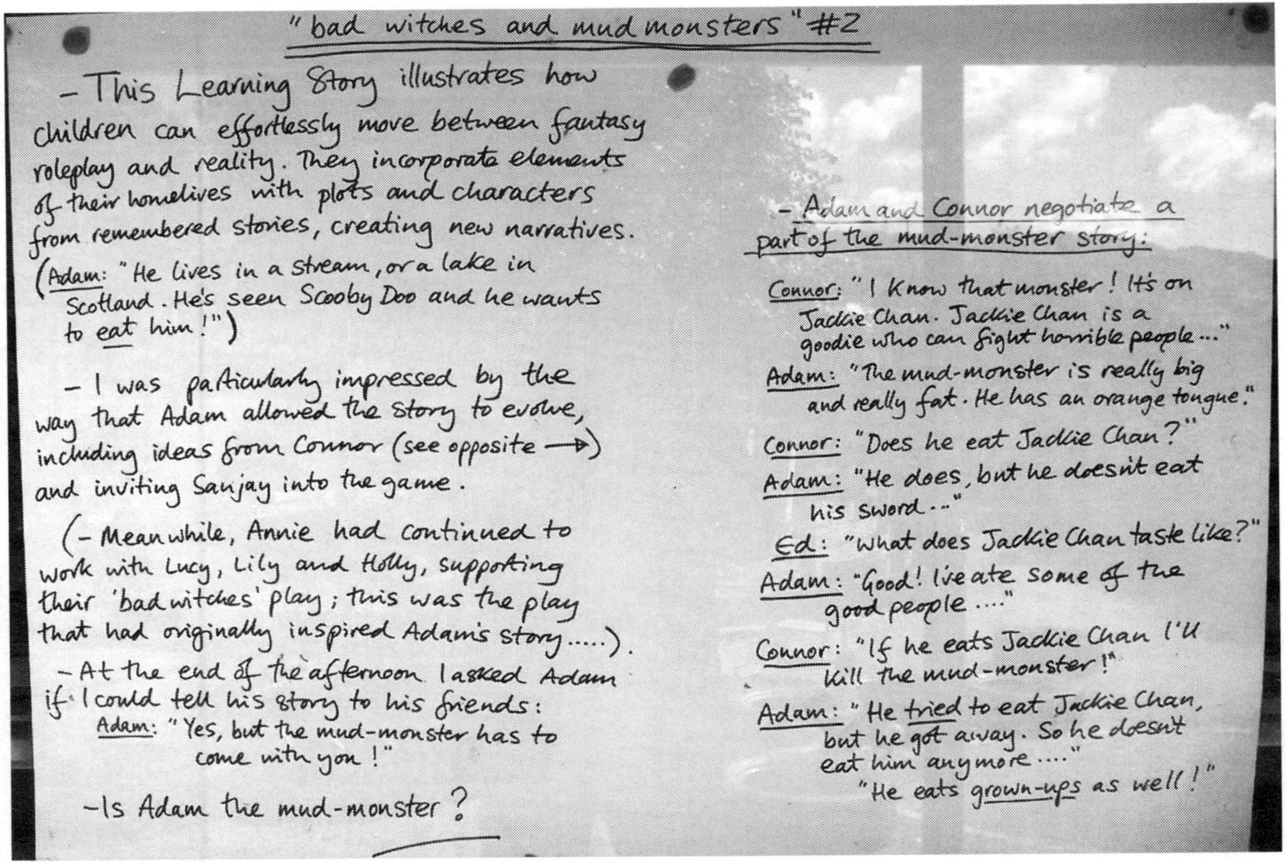

"bad witches and mud monsters" #2

- This Learning Story illustrates how children can effortlessly move between fantasy roleplay and reality. They incorporate elements of their homelives with plots and characters from remembered stories, creating new narratives.

(Adam: "He lives in a stream, or a lake in Scotland. He's seen Scooby Doo and he wants to eat him!")

- I was particularly impressed by the way that Adam allowed the story to evolve, including ideas from Connor (see opposite →) and inviting Sanjay into the game.

(- Meanwhile, Annie had continued to work with Lucy, Lily and Holly, supporting their 'bad witches' play; this was the play that had originally inspired Adam's story.....).

- At the end of the afternoon I asked Adam if I could tell his story to his friends:
Adam: "Yes, but the mud-monster has to come with you!"

- Is Adam the mud-monster?

- Adam and Connor negotiate a part of the mud-monster story:

Connor: "I know that monster! It's on Jackie Chan. Jackie Chan is a goodie who can fight horrible people...."

Adam: "The mud-monster is really big and really fat. He has an orange tongue."

Connor: "Does he eat Jackie Chan?"

Adam: "He does, but he doesn't eat his sword..."

Ed: "What does Jackie Chan taste like?"

Adam: "Good! I've ate some of the good people...."

Connor: "If he eats Jackie Chan I'll kill the mud-monster!"

Adam: "He tried to eat Jackie Chan, but he got away. So he doesn't eat him any more...." "He eats grown-ups as well!"

Figure 9.3: Learning story 2

interpretations of the children's observed behaviour and need to talk them through in order to decide on the next steps. In Reggio this reflective debate is particularly valued. There they place great value on not accepting the 'taken for granted'. In one case, for example, sequences of images showing a ten-month-old girl, Laura, interested in a wristwatch (Edwards *et al.* 1998, pp.116–117), provoked a vigorous discussion among the teachers. First in the sequence, Laura with her carer could be seen looking through a trade catalogue and showing particular interest in the wristwatches illustrated. The carer then held her own wristwatch up to Laura's ear for her to hear the ticking, which brought a thoughtful

Figure 9.4: Documentation on nursery window

expression to the toddler's face. Laura next responded by putting her head down to 'listen' to the image on the page. When this action was discussed by the teachers, some said she was behaving like a scientist, testing out a hypothesis ('Would the image tick?'). Others thought it was not significant, she was just playing.

In creating the documentation its audience must be considered. Who is the documentation for? In reality it becomes a public account for the adult participants, other colleagues and staff in the setting, visitors to the setting including any visiting professionals and researchers, parents, and not least the children themselves who should all have the chance to consider and re-consider the learning stories.

Documentation is indeed about 'making learning visible'. A book with this very title (Giudici *et al.* 2001) was the result of a lengthy combined study from Project Zero set up jointly by Harvard University and Reggio Children (the body responsible for the Reggio preschools). Project Zero identified the key elements of documentation as:

- focused observations
- collective combined group analysis of the observational records
- creation of the documentation, perhaps represented in a variety of forms
- sharing of the documentation with the observed children
- consideration of possible future plans.

The resulting Harvard/Reggio book, *Making Learning Visible*, is highly recommended. Learning stories from toddlers to six-year-olds are included, but it is the background narrative that reveals the processes, situations and thinking that underpin documentation which is so important.

As we have mentioned, sharing and discussing documentation with the observed children is also part of the documentation process, since the children will reveal more of their thinking in subsequent discussion and this in turn can be recorded. How the adults have interpreted the children's ideas can also be checked with them during these discussions. The purpose of documentation is after all to discover the meanings the children attach to their activities. 'The search for the meaning of life is born with the child and is desired by the child' (Giudici *et al.* 2001, p.79). So documentation must be faithful to the experiences and understanding of the learning processes of all involved, children and adults alike.

Documentation is not the same as a 'display'. Quite typically in early years settings every child's painting or other piece of work is carefully mounted, or else a set of captioned photographs are put up on the classroom walls – these are displays and they have their place, but they do not constitute documentation. Display is frequently thought of as celebrating each child's achievement or perhaps recording an activity or event, such as a school trip. Documentation, on the other hand, explicitly invites enquiry about the children's thinking represented in the images and text put on show for everyone to see. It tries to raise questions about the group of children's work together, rather than focusing on each individual's production. As has been explained, the learning stories will reflect the educators' interpretations and probably those of the children as well. Documentation is essential when the adults believe in the shared creation of knowledge and where observations are the subject for dialogue and reflection by those involved. It is a record of the thinking of all, and hence of potential value for further enquiry. For children to see their activity, their visions, their creations and intentions represented and saved for the future in this way, is a powerful validation of their contributions. In evaluating the year's work of 5x5x5, documentation is similarly collected for the insights it supplies about the effect of creative experiences of the children. Each learning story is treasured for its own sake.

Documentation may be described as a kind of ongoing assessment, in that it offers a chance to reflect on the children's work in progress. In New Zealand this method has been adopted in relation to their national guidance, Te Whaariki. Margaret Carr explains the theory and practice in *Assessment in Early Childhood Settings: Learning stories* (2001). (For a thorough study of this approach in Reggio-inspired work see the chapter 'Negotiated learning through design, documentation and discourse' by Forman and Fyfe 1998, pp.239–260 and also Bancroft *et al.* 2008.)

> Once we acknowledge that children are competent thinkers we will need to take an imaginative step into their world, to explore with them the meaning of their logic. This leads us to a much more complex interpretation of their learning experiences. (Sully in Bancroft *et al.* 2008, p.27)

Unfortunately in some educational settings this complexity is never discovered. Children will often be expected to conform to the narrow prescribed topic with no imaginative straying from the path. As a consequence their creative potential, their unique take on things, and their deep emotions may fail to be recognised and affirmed (see Chapter Ten, in particular the case study of Tommy).

Where educators and artists, reflect regularly together on their observations, as in the case of Reggio and 5x5x5, sharing and analysing their personal interpretations in order to understand the children's ideas, this is true research. This more probing critical enquiry serves also to promote continuing personal and professional development.

UNIVERSITY OF WINCHESTER
LIBRARY

CHAPTER TEN

The 'Hundred Languages of Children': Variety in Communicating Meaning

What children say in words matters, but they tell the observer just as much, even more, through other forms of communication, from small gestures to drawing and movement. All their ways of expressing themselves can be called 'languages'. Children move very freely between these different languages, rarely showing consciousness of any divisions. This chapter attempts to discover what may be learned from children as they explore, play, create and communicate their feelings and ideas in such a variety of ways. The first section explains the concept of the hundred languages and its value. The second section gives two examples showing in practical terms what these experiences may mean to the children.

The concept of the hundred languages of children

The phrase the hundred languages of children, which has gone round the world, comes from a poem by Loris Malaguzzi, teacher, psychologist, philosopher, founder and, for many years, the director of the Reggio Emilia preschools (see Chapter Nine). 'Hundred languages' is not to be taken literally. It is a highly significant metaphorical phrase intended to crystallise the idea that children explore and communicate their ideas and feelings in many varied ways, not merely through words. Reggio is not alone, of course, in valuing different forms of expression. Other writers on the subject – and research such as Howard Gardner's 'multiple intelligences' (1999) – emphasise the same idea.

Gunther Kress (1997) uses the word 'multi-modal' to describe a similar principle. For him, in their early years, 'children's ravenous appetite for meaning making leaves no object, no material untouched' (p.33). 'Children experiment, explore, analyse with boundless energy, things which no parent and no school demands' (p.139). He makes the case that many forms of communication are becoming increasingly multi-modal with the arrival of new technologies and indeed all forms of mass media. We are entering a 'new age of hieroglyphics'. Fluent use of all forms of communication of meaning, including visual representations such as diagrams and signs, is already an essential skill, and will be equally necessary to future generations. Yet Kress suggests the overwhelming focus on language and literacy in some early years settings could have serious consequences. The curriculum demands may blind adults to the many other means by which children express themselves, as they imaginatively transform the world around them and adapt any materials and objects that may be at hand. 'Those of their practices which we call "play" we do not consider as part of communication and therefore not worthy of *real* [his italics] investigation' (Kress 1997, p.13). He argues that 'we need to rediscover and reinstate the different possibilities of engagement with the world which are open to us as bodily humans, for all of them offer different, essential modes of being in the world – emotionally, affectively, cognitively' (p.163). It could be said that we are wasting human abilities if we ignore the use of all our potential ways of communicating. We should regard expression through all the senses as highly desirable.

Human communication is rich in its diversity. Clearly the spoken word and its written forms are recognised as of special importance. But speech and writing are only two types of communication, among many others – facial expressions, gestures and body movements, signing, touching, dancing, singing and making music, drawing (two dimensions), constructing (three dimensions), mathematical representations, and using tools like cameras and computers, to mention just a few. These other languages may engage and activate different parts of the brain and involve various 'intelligences' as Gardner (1999) calls them. Each one has its own body of knowledge, perhaps its own symbolic language (for example, musical notation and sign language), and makes its own creative and aesthetic contribution to our culture. Besides much else the different languages enable children to express their imaginative ideas, multi-layered thought, affective emotions, collaborative and interpersonal relationships, and problem-solving. They are obviously not the business of children alone but are indeed part of every person's unconscious taken-for-granted repertoire of self-expression.

The hundred languages in action

A few examples will help to demonstrate how the hundred languages come into play at different stages of a child's development. In their very earliest years children investigate the world through their exploratory drive. This is universally recognised as a fundamental attribute of early childhood – but their intense desire to communicate is not always granted the same significance. From the moment of birth babies engage their carers through their facial expressions. Gopnik and other researchers have shown that babies smile within minutes of birth (Gopnik, Meltzoff and Kuhl 1999). They may imitate their parents in actions such as sticking out their tongue. The youngest infants may also respond visibly to sound. Most people understand the power of music as a way of communicating with babies – think of all those lullabies across the world. Indeed we now know that babies in the womb can hear music and remember it after birth.

Gopnik and her colleagues have confirmed other remarkable competences in babies as they grow. Not only do they explore and express ideas, they also create situations and represent their thoughts, such as imaginatively using a banana as a telephone well before they are a year old. Even two-year-olds have been involved in film-making as documented in research from 5x5x5 (see Chapter Nine). This and many other examples of the capacities of very young children are included in Bancroft *et al.* (2008).

From at least two years of age children energetically interact with everything and anything in their environment. Not confining themselves to simple exploration, they try out ideas and create their own versions of reality through play. Young children have an enviable ability to move between different modes of creative expression. They will make marks with whatever is in reach. During imaginative play they may dance, sing, act out different roles, invent new scenarios and appropriate any likely 'furnishings' such as cushions to build a house. All this happens freely and unselfconsciously (see the Twerton study below). They do not have the mental boundaries that older children gradually acquire, reinforced by a set curriculum and rigid timetables. Creative activity in young children's minds knows no limits. It is not a 30-minute slot on a Wednesday afternoon.

As we have seen, the concept of the hundred languages covers all kinds of expression, but some of these may be of special importance – drawing for instance. Anning and Ring (2004) preface their book on children's drawings with these words: 'When a young child draws they are offering us a window into their own developing understanding of the world and their relationships to significant people, things and places around them'. They start from the premise that children's drawing is 'under-valued, under-researched and misunderstood within the domains of childhood studies and early childhood education'. With its case studies, however, their book shows convincingly that drawing should not be neglected in education. On the contrary 'drawing is a powerful vehicle for hearing what young children are telling us' (p.x).

We often do not know what really matters most to children and young people. Social workers in particular often have to find ways of reaching and understanding children in gravely disturbing situations. In this context, drawing on her work as an arts psychotherapist, Michelle Lefevre places high value on spontaneous play and free image-making. Such activities help children to express their most subjective thoughts and feelings that might otherwise remain repressed and undivulged well beyond the early years. Lefevre writes:

> For some children much of their internal life remains unprocessed and in symbolic form for much longer than might be expected. Some children reach adolescence still with neither the languages to name their experiences nor the conceptual and affective frameworks through which to process them. (Lefevre 2008, p.132)

This publication, an edited collection of articles, covers many important areas of face-to-face work with children. Here the issue of communication is central, with particular regard to communication through the arts. Lefevre indeed refers to the Reggio concept of the hundred languages, and encourages social workers to employ different media, such as drawing, stories and fairy tales, games, creative writing or music, to help children relax and become engaged. Following Lefevre the key points about the arts in communication may be summarised as follows:

- they allow children to express themselves more freely in their own ways and on their own terms

- art forms (of all kinds) offer bridges to open up communication

- that some children may not want to talk about their feelings but will speak through open-ended arts activities (Lefevre, as an arts therapist, particularly uses singing)

- focusing on activities that are real, fun and emotionally warm reduces stress and anxiety.

In particular Lefevre believes in the significance of 'non-directive play', redefining it as 'purposeful activity' rather than dismissing it as 'mere playing' (Lefevre 2008, p.136). Some adults who work with children who have special needs will be acutely aware of the need for alternative means of communication for children to express themselves when they have little or no speech. (A case study of such an approach is given in Bancroft *et al.* 2008, p.113.) The hundred languages concept empowers children and adults too, as they build relationships and forge their sense of self. Inventiveness is intricately linked with expression and must surely count among the most important capacities to be nourished if people are to deal with the challenges they meet throughout life. Anna Craft has spoken of 'life-wide creativity', a very broad capacity that includes the notion of 'possibility thinking' (Craft 2002). That means the ability to think 'out of the box' and consider possibilities from all types of experience. Keeping an open mind and constantly experimenting, rather than sticking to a fixed approach, seems to be relatively natural to most children. Malaguzzi, as already mentioned, always insisted on seeing children's actions from the child's angle:

> [Children] are not excessively attached to their own ideas, which they construct and reinvent continuously. They are apt to explore, make discoveries, change their points of view, and fall in love with forms and meanings that transform themselves. (Malaguzzi 1998, p.75)

The hundred languages matter in many other ways too. It is part of the Reggio philosophy that in order to promote learning, children should be able to employ diverse modes of expression when pursuing their story lines since they stimulate different parts of the brain and encourage flexibility of mind. *Revisiting* is a key concept in their learning process, when the children are helped to recall earlier ideas or activities. Hearing children's explanations and interpretations brings greater understanding of the original experience.

A wonderful series of chapters demonstrating this process can be found in Reggio Children's most recent publication concerning the children's response to the new Loris Malaguzzi International Centre

(Filippini, Giudici and Vecchi 2008). Each local preschool first made a separate reconnoitring visit to the Centre and the children's reactions to the architectural spaces were recorded in photographs, video and notes. Back in the preschool the children 'revisited' their experiences with the help of elaborate digital technology. Their task was then for each pre-school to make some sort of 'present' for the new building. In one case the children came up with the notion that a small creature (a ladybird) lived in the space at the top of a column at the Centre. This led into an observational and biological study of ladybirds and imaginative stories about the insect's journeys. Finally they transformed the column into 'the most beautiful house' for the ladybird. They made a huge collage repre-senting flowers, leaves, etc., which was then photographed. The resulting large strips of the beautiful design were eventually wrapped round the column at the Centre itself (Filippini *et al.* 2008, pp.80–88).

Two examples of the hundred languages in action from 5x5x5

In 5x5x5 (see Chapter Nine) many observations or 'learning stories' have been collected showing children moving seamlessly between the various modes of expression, as in the first case study below. The second concerns the expression of very deep feelings about bereavement.

Twerton case study

Amy, a visual artist from 5x5x5, had become a regular feature of the school (situated in an area of predominantly council housing) and had worked with the reception class of four- to five-year-olds each year for the last five years. She described herself to me as an artist 'using anima-tion, video and porcelain to explore the hidden and revealed histories and stories related to old textiles and photographs placed in the context of our lives in the present'.

A visit to the 'egg', a children's theatre in Bath, to see *Petrushka* per-formed with puppets to Stravinsky's music seemed initially, at the event itself, to be making little impression on the children – despite being an enjoyable expedition. One week later Amy arrived with a large suitcase full of 'tantalising materials, including pea sticks, cups, buttons, and fabrics…'. She also brought along hats and music CDs and created a screened area in the classroom similar to that used in the *Petrushka* perfor-mance. The suitcase intrigued the children, but only gradually did they

10.1 puppet

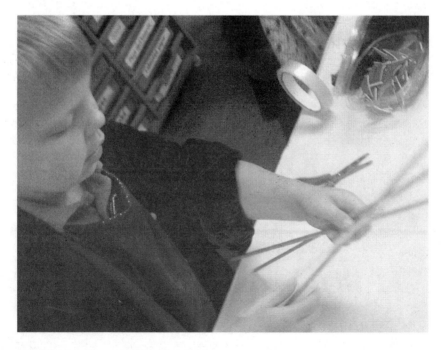

10.2 Alex starting to model with peasticks

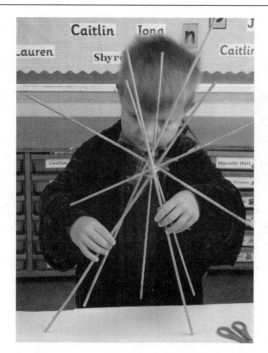

10.3 Alex, completed star

10.4 Rhia and Louise on keboard

discover the potential of the resources for their creative play. It began with Rhia working completely on her own initiative, 'quietly and discreetly', making a puppet from a cup (at the show the children had each been given a cup to make a puppet). She spent most of the morning on her construction, seeking only a little adult help with a roll of Sellotape. Other children then began using the pea sticks to make kites which then evolved into puppets. Alex (who according to the teacher rarely 'makes things') next became very involved and started creating a star structure out of the pea sticks. He sustained this for 25 minutes and kept returning to it throughout the day. At intervals he tried to make it stand up.

Parallel with the puppet-making, which gradually took off across the class, the children began to explore the possibilities of music-making to assist with what they termed their 'shows' (following the theatre visit). The musical theme progressed over the next few weeks. From sound-making with glasses containing different quantities of water, and elastic bands stretched over boxes and other containers, the music progressed to a real guitar and electric keyboard. The children led the way, and even though the artist claimed not to have any musical expertise she thoughtfully created an environment in which the children were able to

10.5 Klajdi and guitar

explore the intriguing world of sound further. She discovered that the class teacher could play the piano so the children capitalised on this lucky chance. Rhia wanted to write in musical notation. 'I have a piano at home and I was wondering if I could do some notes to play a proper song.' The class teacher showed her how to draw stavelines and write notes, explaining what the stavelines and notes meant. Rhia spent a long time writing her own music and Louise also became interested and joined in. Later, in the school garden, the electric keyboard was set up and the two girls continued their writing and playing.

Meanwhile Klajdi was intrigued by the guitar (and continued to be so over the next few weeks). He explored different ways of listening to the guitar as he plucked the strings and, unusually, he became very attentive to other sounds in the environment, especially a blackbird singing in bushes near the children.

Klajdi: I want to find out why do birds sing?

Amy: Why do you think they sing?

Klajdi: 'Cos they're happy and excited.

Klajdi: Everyone's attention please!

He calls to the birds: Birds attention please!

Caitlin: They still can't hear you.

Then Klajdi spoke to the hole in the guitar: Hello, hello, Mr Hole!

In summary, constructing the puppets led on to wanting to stage a show, for which the children decided they needed music. So they improvised musical instruments, and two also wanted to write music down while others took on roles as compères and directors. Meanwhile Klajdi responded to the situation by continuing his own musical enquiries into the potential of the guitar.

St Stephens School study of Tommy

In 5x5x5 practice impetus for the children's activities arises out the children's own ideas. The adults always begin by observing and recording what the children do for several weeks before they choose a theme around which the children's thinking can coalesce. The process is then supported by placing sufficient 'intelligent materials' (open-ended basic resources) at their disposal and by attentive observation followed by meetings for joint reflection and discussion – the 'documentation' part (see Chapter Nine).

St Stephen's Church of England primary school had already been involved in 5x5x5 for two years. The visual artist, Linda, who 'paints, draws and makes', was working with the two large reception classes of four- to five-year-old children. Each week she took small groups of children out of the classroom into the 'drama hall'. She provided them with a variety of mark-making options such as felt-tip pens, crayons, pencils and poster paint, and a range of paper, large and small. She also supplied an assortment of fabrics, netting and other materials from Scrapstore (an organisation offering off-cuts and odds and ends from factories) plus a variety of pictures (including some from Linda's own collection). The following case study shows how some of these materials helped a child come to terms with his profound feelings. It concerns four-year-old Tommy. Just before Linda began the 5x5x5 work with this year group, Tommy's much-loved grandfather had died not long after the death of his other grandmother. Tommy had attended the funerals, but it was the family gatherings afterwards that seemed to have specially impressed him. Initial observations had suggested he was a capable, quite articulate child. He claimed, however, that he couldn't draw pictures, though he did draw maps and would use these and other images to tell stories. Linda described him as 'very emotionally intelligent with a somewhat preoccupied calm demeanour'. A pirate theme evolved in the group of children, particularly among the boys, and a large boat built from chicken wire and plaster of Paris was created. Tommy was much absorbed in the painting of the boat, choosing black for the major part and then adding red – 'the blood'. He said the boat was 'a hundred, thousand, thousand years old' and tried to paint this number on the boat's side. He made a number of books during these sessions. On one occasion he quietly gathered together paper and a few old postcards (depicting historical royal palaces) and started making another book.

I'm fascinated in books, in funeral books. The cards remind me of my Dad's Dad.

I went to my Dad's Mum's house and loads of people came to my Dad's Mum's house. I can't really remember what happened then. I'm going to save some pictures for my Mum and Dad. I'm saving that one, not this one, because it's like a funeral [a picture of cups and saucers]. The cups and saucers remind me, because usually people eat afterwards ... Jesus got crucified. I used to say my Grandma got crucified, so I'm making a funeral book. This reminds me of the funeral. I'm cutting the paper, it's too big, and the pictures won't fit in. I'm not going to draw it, I've got to fold it, so it's a funeral book ... [He finds some shells] They might be interesting to put on the front page, stuck with sellotape. There! I've drawn my face. [He wrote 'Author by Tommy']

The book and pictures tell me about my Dad's Dad.

[He then went to the clay table and modelled a pirate ship out of the clay.]

At the end of the year the documentation from all the sessions with the St Stephen's artist – children's drawings, constructions, photographs, the text of the children's dialogue and some of the adults' comments – were displayed at their cultural centre for parents, teachers and friends to see, enjoy and learn from. Tommy's father looked closely at his son's books and words, clearly moved, and father and son spent some time talking quietly together. Later the father told the artist how very surprised he was – 'I thought Tommy was quite sporty, I didn't know he had this side to him. He has never shown it at home.'

10.6 Tommy's book cover

In the evaluation session with the class teacher she too expressed surprise, having had no idea about the depth of Tommy's feelings and knowledge. All the staff, including the headteacher, remarked on the significance of the 5x5x5 experience for Tommy. The class teacher felt that having the artist in the school had a 'chemical effect' similar to yeast in flour. 'She loves the children, supports and respects their ideas, she works alongside them allowing them time.' In the 5x5x5 sessions at St Stephen's the children participate with the artist in a fairly small group and can follow ideas through, taking advantage of the rich opportunities on offer in a non-judgemental atmosphere. In a large busy class with lots of distraction a child like Tommy would probably not have had the psychological space to reveal this sensitive side of his nature and to express the deep feelings aroused by bereavement.

10.7 A spontaneous drawing by Lily (4 years old), done at home after a 5x5x5 day at school

UNIVERSITY OF WINCHESTER
LIBRARY

10.8 From St Stephen's reception class following zoo visit

10.9 From St Stephen's reception class following zoo visit

Conclusion

Allowing children access to 'a hundred languages' may at first sight appear to be all about giving them stimulating opportunities for play. This is true up to a point, but there is much more to it than that. The adults are key players even if they do refrain from over-zealous intervention in the children's actions. It is they who contribute the essential ingredients:

- seeing children as 'meaning-makers'
- creating a thoughtful, enabling environment
- offering open-ended 'intelligent materials'
- allowing children to transform these materials
- being attentive to and supporting the children's ideas
- recording the experiences
- reflecting, with others, on the experience to create documentation.

Lefevre (2008) warns against seeing these experiences as play therapy, the domain of the professional therapist. But all professionals concerned with children can appreciate the extra dimensions offered by a very wide range of communicative forms – 'the hundred is there' as the poem says. Even in very informal ways, and without the benefit of the artists of Reggio and 5x5x5, any worker with young children can facilitate their willing creativity.

Appendix: The task code categories from the Oxford Preschool Research Project

The Target Child method has a column labelled TASK which refers to the kind of activity the child is engaged in. These activities may consist of a particular task or type of play but the list below also includes non-play and other ways a child may be spending the time.

Large muscle movement – LMM: Active movement, such as climbing, running, jumping, using the larger muscles.

Large-scale construction – LSC: Building with planks, PVC covered soft blocks, big boxes and bricks, etc.

Small-scale construction – SSC: Using small-scale construction materials such as Lego, Mobilo and Sticklebricks.

Scale-version toys – SVT: Organising small-scale objects such as toy cars, zoo or farm animals. If the toys are being used in pretend play, use the next category.

Pretend or imaginative play – PRE: Using objects 'as if' they are something else.

Structured materials – SM: Using materials with a particular purpose, e.g. jigsaw puzzles, peg-boards, shape posting boxes, bead-threading.

Art – ART: Drawing, painting, junk-modelling, cutting and sticking.

Manipulation – MAN: Mastering or refining skills which require hand–eye co-ordination, e.g. handling sand, dough, clay, water, etc. Also includes sewing and gardening.

Adult-directed craft and manipulation – ADM: Adults guiding and directing children (sometimes with an adult-determined end product), e.g. in the making of festive cards, tracing, directed collage, etc.

Three Rs Activities – 3Rs: Making attempts at reading, writing or mathematics.

Examination – EX: Examining an object or material with care, e.g. looking through a magnifying glass.

Problem-solving – PS: Trying to solve a problem in a logical way, e.g. looking to see why something will not work and trying to put it right.

Games with rules – GWR: Playing ball games, circle and singing games, board games such as Lotto or Snakes and Ladders.

Informal games – IG: Playing spontaneously, e.g. loosely organised games between two or more children, following each other around, chanting, holding hands and jumping.

Music – MUS: Listening to any kind of music, playing instruments, singing as a group or alone.

Passive adult-led group activities – PALGA: Adult leading a large group of children, e.g. stories, finger rhymes, watching television, or demonstrating (e.g. how to plant seeds).

Social interaction, non-play – SINP: This category is used only when a child is not engaged in any of the other task code categories. It covers social interaction with another child or adult, verbal or non-verbal, e.g. chatting, seeking help, teasing, being comforted by an adult.

Distress behaviour – DB: The child is visibly distressed and seeking comfort or attention from an adult or a child.

Standing around, aimless wander or gaze – SA/AWG: The child is not actively engaged in a task or watching something specific.

Cruise – CR: 'Butterfly' behaviour, the child may appear to be searching for something to do.

Purposeful movement – PM: The child moves with deliberate intention towards a person, place or object, e.g. looking for a piece of equipment, going outdoors.

Wait – W: The child is inactive, waiting for an adult or child.

Watching – WA: The child is watching other people or events, listening in to conversations, but not participating.

Domestic activity – DA: This category includes going to the toilet, hand-washing, arriving and departing, snacks and meals.

The above categories have been adapted from Sylva *et al.* (1980), pp.240–243.

References

Abbott, L. and Langston, A. (eds) (2005) *Birth to Three Matters*. Buckingham: Open University Press.

Anning, A., Cottrell, D.M., Frost, N., Green, J. and Robinson, M. (2006) *Developing Multiprofessional Teamwork for Integrated Children's Services: Research and policy*. Maidenhead: Open University Press.

Anning, A. and Ring, K. (2004) *Making Sense of Children's Drawings*. Maidenhead: Open University Press.

Athey, C. (1990) *Extending Thought in Young Children: A parent–teacher partnership*. London: Paul Chapman Publishing.

Baldwin, M. (1994) 'Why observe children?' *Social Work Education 13*, 2, 74–85.

Barker, R.G. and Wright, H.F. (1951) *One Boy's Day: A specimen record of behavior*. New York: Harper.

Blurton-Jones, N. (ed) (1972) *Ethological Studies of Child Behaviour*. Cambridge: Cambridge University Press.

Bowlby, J. (1951) *Maternal Care and Mental Health*. Geneva: World Health Organisation.

Bowlby, J. (1969) *Attachment and Loss: Vol. 1. Attachment*. London: Hogarth Press.

Bradley, B.S. (1989) *Visions of Infancy*. Oxford: Basil Blackwell.

Briggs, S. (1992) 'Child observation and social work training.' *Journal of Social Work Practice 6*, 1, 49–61.

Briggs, S. (1999) 'Links between infant observation and reflective social work practice.' *Journal of Social Work Practice* 13:2.

Bronfenbrenner, U. (1979) *The Ecology of Human Development*. Cambridge, MA: Harvard University Press.

Bruner, J. (1975) 'Nature and Uses of Immaturity.' In J.S. Bruner, A. Jolly and K. Sylva (eds) *Play: Its role in development and evolution*. Harmondsworth: Penguin.

Carr, M. (2001) *Assessment in Early Childhood Settings: Learning stories*. London: Paul Chapman Publishing.

Carr, M. and Claxton, G. (2004) 'A framework for teaching learning: The dynamics of disposition.' *Early Years 24*, 1, 87–97.

Carruthers, E. and Worthington, M. (2006) *Children's Mathematics: Making marks, making meaning* (2nd edition). London: Sage Publications.

Clark, A. and Moss, P. (2001) *Listening to Young Children: The mosaic approach.* London: National Children's Bureau.

Craft, A. (2002) *Creativity and the Early Years: A lifewide foundation.* London: Continuum.

Csikszentmihalyi, M. (2002) *Flow.* London: Rider.

Darwin, C. (1859) *On the Origin of Species.* London: John Murray.

Darwin, C. (1872) *The Expression of Emotions in Man and Animals.* London: John Murray.

Darwin, C. (1877) 'A biographical sketch of an infant.' *Mind 7,* 285–294, reprinted in W. Kessen (1965) *The Child: Perspectives in Psychology.* New York: John Wiley.

David, T., Goouch, K., Powell, S. and Abbott, L. (2003) *Birth to Three Matters: A review of the literature (DFES Research Report No. 444).* London: Department for Education and Skills. Available at www.surestart.gov.uk/_doc/0-9916C.pdf

Department for Children, Schools and Families (DCSF) (2007a) *Care Matters: Time for change* (Cm7137). White Paper. London: The Stationery Office. Accessed 05/11/08 at http://publications.dcsf.gov.uk

Department for Children, Schools and Families (DCSF) (2007b) *The Children's Plan.* London: The Stationery Office.

Department for Education and Skills (2003) *Every Child Matters: Change for children* (Cm 5860) London: The Stationery Office.

Department for Education and Skills (2004) *Choice for Parents, the Best Start for Children: A ten-year strategy for childcare.* London: DfES. Accessed 23/10/08. at www.everychildmatters.gov.uk/earlyyears/tenyearstrategy/

Department for Education and Skills (2005) *Common Assessment Framework.* London: DfES. Accessed 23/10/08 at www.everychildmatters.gov.uk/deliveringservices/cap/

Diwidi, K.N. (ed) (2002) *Meeting the Needs of Ethnic Minority Children Including Refugee, Black and Mixed Parentage Children: A Handbook for Professionals.* 2nd Edition. London: Jessica Kingsley Publishers.

Dixon, B. (1989) *Playing them False: A study of children's toys, games and puzzles.* Stoke-on-Trent: Trentham Books.

Doddington, C. and Hilton, M. (2007) *Child-centred Education: Reviving the creative tradition.* London: Sage Publications.

Donaldson, M. (1978) *Children's Minds.* Glasgow: Fontana.

Drummond, M.J. (1993) *Assessing Children's Learning.* London: David Fulton.

Drummond, M.J., Rouse, D. and Pugh, G. (1992) *Making Assessment Work: Values and principles in assessing young children.* London: NES Arnold in association with National Children's Bureau.

Dunn, J. (1988) *The Beginnings of Social Understanding.* Oxford: Basil Blackwell.

Dunn, J. (1993) *Children's Close Relationships: Beyond attachment.* London: Sage Publications.

Elfer, P. and Dearnley, K. (2007) 'Nurseries and emotional well-being: Evaluating an emotionally containing model of professional development.' *Early Years 27,* 3, 267–279.

Elfer, P., Goldschmied, E. And Selleck, D. (2003) *Key Persons in the Nursery: Building relationships for quality provision.* London: David Fulton.

Elfer, P. and Selleck, D. (1999) 'Children under three in nurseries 'Uncertainty as a creative factor in child observation' *European Early Childhood Education Research Journal 7,* 1, 69–82.

Engel, S.L. (2005) *Real Kids: Creating meaning in everyday life.* Cambridge, MA: Harvard University Press.

Filippini, T., Giudici, C. and Vecchi, V. (curators) (2008) *Dialogues with Places: The exhibition.* Reggio Emilia, Italy: Reggio Children.

Forman, G. and Fyfe, B. (1998) 'Negotiated learning through Design, Documentation, and Discourse.' In C. Edwards, L. Gandini and G. Forman (eds) *The Hundred Languages of Children: The Reggio Emilia Approach – Advanced Reflections* (2nd edition). Westport, CT: Ablex Publishing.

Gambe, D., Gomes, J., Kapur, V., Rongel, M. and Stubbs, P. (1992) *Improving Practice with Children and Families: A training manual.* London: Northern Curriculum Development Project (CCETSW, Leeds).

Gandini, L. (1998) In C. Edwards, L. Gandini and G. Forman (eds) (1998) *The Hundred Languages of Children: The Reggio Emilia Approach – Advanced Reflections* (2nd edition). Westport, CT: Ablex Publishing.

Gardner, H. (1999) *Frames of Mind.* Cambridge, MA: Harvard University Press.

Gerhardt, S. (2004) *Why Love Matters: How affection shapes a baby's brain.* London: Routledge.

Gittins, D. (1998) *The Child in Question.* London: Macmillan Press.

Giudici, C., Rinaldi, C. and Krechevsky, M. (2001) *Making Learning Visible: Children as individual and group learners.* Cambridge, MA: Harvard University and Reggio Emilia: Reggio Children.

Gonzalez-Mena, J. (1993) *Multicultural Issues in Child Care.* Mountian View, CA: Mayfield Publishing Company.

Gopnik, A., Meltzoff, A. and Kuhl, P. (1999) *How Babies Think: The science of childhood.* London: Weidenfeld and Nicholson.

Gurian, M. (2001) *Boys and Girls Learn Differently: A guide for teachers and parents.* San Francisco, CA: Jossey-Bass.

Gussin Paley, V. (2004) *A Child's Work: The importance of fantasy play.* Chicago, IL: University of Chicago Press.

Hallden, G. (1991) 'The child as project and the child as being: Parents' ideas as frames of reference.' *Children and Society 5,* 4, 334–46.

Harcourt, D. and Conroy, H. (2005) 'Informed assent: ethics and processes when researching young children.' *Early Child Development and Care 175,* 6, 566–77.

Harris, P.L. (1994) The child's understanding of emotion: Developmental change and the family environment.' *Journal of Psychology and Psychiatry 35,* 1, 3–28.

Harrison, F. (1985) *A Father's Diary.* London: Fontana, Flamingo.

Hazareesingh, S., Simms, K. and Anderson, P. (1989) *Educating the Whole Child: A holistic approach to education in the early years.* London: Building Blocks (Save the Children).

Hendrick, H. (1997) 'Constructions and reconstructions of British Childhood: An interpretive survey 1800 to the present.' In A. James and A. Prout (eds) *Constructing and Reconstructing Childhood: Contemporary Issues in the Sociological Study of Childhood.* London: Falmer Press.

Henshall, C. and McGuire, J. (1986) 'Gender Development' in M. Richards and P. Light (eds) *Children of Social Worlds.* Oxford: Basil Blackwell.

Her Majesty's Treasury (HMT) (2004) *Choice for Parents, the Best Start for Children: A ten year strategy for childcare.* London: The Stationery Office.

Isaacs, S. (1930) *Intellectual Growth in Young Children.* London: Routledge, Kegan Paul.

Isaacs, S. (1933) *Social Development in Young Children.* London: Routledge, Kegan Paul.

Jackson, S. and Fawcett, M. (2009) 'Early childhood policy and services.' In T. Maynard and N. Thomas (eds) *An Introduction to Early Childhood Studies* (2nd edition). London: Sage publications.

Johnson, M. (2007) *Wasted.* Little, Brown Book Group.

Kessen, W. (1965) *The Child: Perspectives in psychology.* New York: John Wiley.

Kress, G. (1997) *Before Writing: Rethinking paths to literacy.* London: Routledge.

Laming, Lord (2003) *The Victoria Climbié Inquiry Report.* London: The Stationery Office.

Laevers, F. (1994) *The Leuven Involvement Scale for Young Children.* Leuren, Belgum Centre for Experiential Education.

Laevers, F. (2000) 'Forward to the Basics! Deep-Level-Learning and the Experiential Approach.' *Early Years, 20,* 2, 20–29. Leuven University Belgium: Centre for Experiential Education.

Lefevre, M. (2008) 'Communicating and engaging with children and young people in care through play and the creative arts.' In B. Luckock and M. Lefevre (eds) *Direct Work: Social work with children and young people in care.* London: BAAF.

Le Riche, P. and Tanner, K. (eds) (1998) *Observation and its Application to Social Work: Rather like breathing.* London: Jessica Kingsley Publishers.

Luckock, B. and Lefevre, M. (eds) (2008) *Direct Work: Social work with children and young people in care.* London: BAAF.

Luckock, B., Lefevre, M., Orr, D., Jones, M., Marchant, R. and Tanner, K. (2006) *Knowledge Review 12, Teaching and Learning and Assessing Communication Skills in Social Work Education.* Social Care Institute for Excellence. Accessed April 2008 at www.scie.org.uk/publications.

Malaguzzi, L. (1998) in Edwards, C., Gandini, L. and Forman, G. (eds) *The Hundred Languages of Children: The Reggio Emilia Approach – Advanced Reflections.* Westport, CT: Ablex.

McGrew, W.C. (1972) *An Ethological Study of Children's Behaviour.* New York and London: Academic Press.

Miller, L., Rustin, Margaret, Rustin, Michael and Shuttleworth, J. (eds) (1989) *Closely Observed Infants.* London: Duckworth.

Moyles, J. (ed) (1989) *Just Playing? The role and status of play in early childhood education.* Milton Keynes: Open University Press.

Moyles, J. (ed) (1994) *The Excellence of Play.* Milton Keynes: Open University.

New Zealand Ministry of Education (1996) *Te Whaariki; Early Childhood Curriculum.* Wellington, New Zealand: Learning Media.

Noyes, P. for the Department of Health (1991) *Child Abuse: A study of inquiry reports.* London: HMSO.

Nutbrown, C. (2006a) *Key Concepts in Early Childhood Education and Care.* London: Sage Publications.

Nutbrown, C. (2006b) *Threads of Thinking: Young children learning and the role of early education* (3rd edition). London: Sage Publications.

Ofsted (Office for Standards in Education) (2003) *The Education of Six year olds in England, Denmark and Finland: An international comparative study.* London: Ofsted Publications.

Owen, S. (2006) 'Training and workforce issues.' In G. Pugh and B. Duffy (eds) *Contemporary Issues in the Early Years* (4th edition). London: Sage Publications.

Owusu-Bempah, J. (1994) 'Race, self-identity and social work.' *British Journal of Social Work 24,* 123–136.

Parten, M. (1933) 'Social play among preschool children.' *Journal of Abnormal and Social Psychology 28*, 136–147.

Pascal, C. and Bertram, T. (1997) *Effective Early Learning: Case studies in improvement.* London: Hodder and Stoughton.

Pease, A. (1981) *Body Language: How to read others' thoughts by their gestures.* London: Sheldon Press.

Petrie, P., Boddy, J., Cameron, C., Heptinstall, E., McQuail, S. and Simon, A. (2008) *Pedagogy – a Holistic, Personal Approach to Work with Children and Young People across Services: European models for practice, training, education and qualification.* London: Tomas Coram Research Unit, Institute for Education, University of London.

Pinker, S. (1994) *The Language Instinct.* Harmondsworth: Penguin.

Qualifications and Curriculum Authority (2000) *Foundation Stage Guidance.* London Qualification and Curriculum Authority.

Rinaldi, C. (2006) *In Dialogue with Reggio Emilia: Listening, researching and learning.* London: Routledge.

Rogoff, B. (1990) *Apprenticeship in Thinking: Cognitive development in a social context.* New York: Oxford University Press.

Rogoff, B. (2003) *The Cultural Nature of Human Development.* Oxford: Oxford University Press.

Rousseau, J-J. (1975) *Emile, or On Education* (English translation). New York: Basic Books. (Original work published 1762.)

Rustin, M. (1989) 'Encountering primitive anxieties.' In L. Miller, M. Rustin and J. Shuttleworth (eds) *Closely Observed Infants.* London: Duckworth.

Rutter, M. (1972) *Maternal Deprivation Reassessed.* Harmondsworth: Penguin.

Schön, D. (1987) *Educating the Reflective Practitioner: Toward a new design for teaching and learning in the professions.* San Francisco, CA: Jossey Bass.

Sheridan, M. (1973) *Children's Developmental Progress from Birth to Five.* London: NFER. (Original work published 1960.)

Siraj-Blatchford, I. (1994) *The Early Years: Laying the foundations for racial equality.* Stoke-on-Trent: Trentham Books.

Siraj-Blatchford, I. (2007) *The Team around the Child: Multi-agency working in the early years.* Stoke-on-Trent: Trentham Books.

Siraj-Blatchford, I. (2009) 'Early Childhood Education.' In T. Maynard and N. Thomas (eds) *An Introduction to Early Childhood Studies* (2nd edition). London: Sage Publications.

Siraj-Blatchford, I., Sylva, K., Muttock, S., Gilden, R. and Bell, D. (2002) *Researching Effective Pedagogy in the Early Years (REPEY).* London: HMSO.

Sully, A. (2008) 'The role of documentation'. In Bancroft, S., Fawcett, M. and Hay, P. (eds) *Researching Children Researching the World: 5x5x5=creativity.* Stoke-on-Trent: Trentham Books.

Sylva, K., Melhuish, E.C., Sammons, P., Siraj-Blatchford, I. and Taggart, B. (2004) *The Effective Provision of Pre-school Education (EPPE) Project: Final Report.* London: DfES/Institute of Education, University of London.

Sylva, K., Roy, C. and Painter, M. (1980) *Childwatching at Playgroup and Nursery School.* London: Grant McIntyre.

Thorne, B. (1993) *Gender Play: Girls and boys in school.* Buckingham: Open University Press.

Tizard, B. and Hughes, M. (1984) *Young Children Learning: Talking and thinking at home and school.* London: Fontana Paperbacks.

Tobin, J.J., David, Y.H. Wu and Davidson, D.H. (1989) *Preschool in Three Cultures: Japan, China and the United States.* NewHaven: Yale University Press.

Turney, D. (2008) 'The power of the gaze: Observation and its role in direct practice with children in care.' In B. Luckock and M. Lefevre (eds) *Direct Work with Children and Young People in Care.* London: British Association for Adoption and Fostering.

United Nations (1989) *Convention on the Rights of the Child.* New York: United Nations.

Wells, G. (1987) *The Meaning Makers: Children learning language and using language to learn.* London: Hodder and Stoughton.

Welsh Assembly Government (2008) *Foundation Phase: Framework for Children's Learning for 3 to 7-year-olds in Wales.* Accessed 23.10.08 at www.wales.gov.uk/topics/educationandskills/policy–strategy–and–planning/104009-wag/foundation–phase/?1

Wertsch J.V. and Addison Stone, C. 'The concenpt of Internalization in Vygotsky's Account of the Genesis of Higher Mental Function'. In Wertsch, J.V. (ed) (1985) *Culture, Communication and Cognition: Vygotskian perspectives.* Cambridge: Cambridge University Press.

WGARCR (1991) *Guidelines for the Selection and Evaluation of Child Development Books.* London: Working Group Against Racism in Children's Resources (460 Wandsworth Road, London, SW8 3LX).

Woodhead, M. and Faulkner, D. (2000) 'Subjects, objects or participants? Dilemmas of psychological research.' In P. Christensen and A. James (eds) *Research with Children: Perspectives and Practice.* London: Routledge Falmer.

Subject Index

Author Index

UNIVERSITY OF WINCHESTER
LIBRARY

UNIVERSITY OF WINCHESTER
LIBRARY